# THEORY OF KNOWLEDGE

## AN INTRODUCTION

A. D. Woozley

Professor of Philosophy
at the University of Virginia

HUTCHINSON OF LONDON

Hutchinson & Co (Publishers) Ltd
3 Fitzroy Square, London W1

London Melbourne Sydney Auckland
Wellington Johannesburg and agencies
throughout the world

First published 1949
Reprinted 1957, 1959, 1960, 1962
1964, 1966, 1969, 1973, 1976 and 1978

Printed in Great Britain by litho by The Anchor Press Ltd
and bound by Wm Brendon & Son Ltd
both of Tiptree, Essex

ISBN 0 09 044572 4 (paper)

56

# THEORY OF KNOWLEDGE

Philosophy

Editor

PROFESSOR S. KÖRNER
jur.Dr., Ph.D., F.B.A.
Professor of Philosophy
University of Bristol and Yale University

# CONTENTS

# PREFACE

I do not see how a book can serve to introduce non-experts to philosophy unless it is elementary. Therefore that this book is elementary and covers much already well-worked ground I impenitently confess. Much of it is devoted to dealing with theories and arguments which I hold to be false, and to showing why I hold them to be false. I have thought it more important to exhibit ways of philosophical thinking and discussion (even though some of them may be thought to be outmoded) than to arrive at definite conclusions. I have judged it to be the main purpose of this series to suggest to readers what are some of the problems of philosophy, and to indicate methods of tackling them. Within the limits available it has not been possible both to carry out that programme and to provide carefully tailored solutions to the questions raised. Nothing better than reach-me-down answers can be hoped for, where answers are offered at all. If they help to cultivate the beginner's taste for *haute couture* in philosophy, the object of the book will have been achieved. Practised philosophers have nothing to gain by reading it.

My thanks are due to Professor H. J. Paton, Mr H. H. Cox, and to Mr H. P. Grice, each of whom read the whole of or part of the manuscript and made many helpful criticisms, from which I have tried to profit; and to Mr B. G. Mitchell, who relieved me of the tedious task of compiling the index.

*February, 1949*                                                    A.D.W.

# I

## INTRODUCTORY

### 1. Theories require questions

Any theory is an answer or set of answers to a question or set of questions; and answers can be unhelpful either because they are incorrect, or correct but unclear, or because the questions prompting them are unclear. The mother who diagnoses her child's spots as measles is producing a theory; if she supposes the child has measles because she knows he has been in contact at school with other children who have developed measles, she is producing reasons in favour of her theory. The doctor who suggests that the spots are symptomatic not of measles but of acidity is producing a rival theory; if he supposes it because the child shows no other symptoms of measles, but has on the other hand been recently eating large quantities of plums, he is producing reasons for his theory; and if after treatment suitable to his diagnosis, e.g. by dosing the child with bicarbonate of soda and by cutting plums and possibly other fruit out of his diet, the spots then disappear, we would normally say that the doctor's theory had been proved correct, and the mother's theory wrong.

That is a simple and straightforward case where the question was clear, 'What is the cause of my child's spots?' and where the rival answers were clear, 'Measles' and 'No, not measles, but acidity,' and where a decision between the rival answers can be made without much difficulty. Other cases can be far less straightforward, e.g. where the symptoms are not visible but internal, and where the patient cannot describe them clearly enough for the doctor to be sure exactly what question it is that he is supposed to be answering. Faced with little and possibly misleading information, the doctor has to indulge in more or less intelligent guesswork, and to try out alternative guesses in turn, until the trouble clears up; and even when it has, the doctor may not have produced a satisfactory theory about it, either because he is not sure which of the various treatments that he tried out did the trick (or even whether any of them did it), or because he still is not sure exactly what the trick was that he had been called on to do.

Now, one of the major difficulties facing anyone starting philosophy is to see what the questions are. And, indeed, many of the difficulties in which trained and experienced philosophers involve themselves are due, according to their fellow philosophers who criticise their theories, to their not being clear enough in the first place just what questions they were setting out to answer; if only they had been clearer about that, the criticism continues, they would have seen either that the questions which they were trying to answer were different from the questions which they *thought* they were trying to answer, or that there was really no question there at all and that it was only their own confusion which made them think that there was a question. As we shall see,[1] this criticism contains more than a grain of truth. Philosophy, indeed, sometimes seems to its practitioners to be a nightmare game of Snakes and Ladders in which the pattern of the board behind you is constantly changing, so that when you land on a snake and slide down it to a square where you were before, you find that the square is disturbingly different from what it was when you were there last time, and so are all the neighbouring squares.

## 2. What are the questions about knowledge?

What, then, are the questions which that branch of philosophy commonly known as the Theory of Knowledge is designed to answer? Or, rather, what are the questions which rival theories in that branch of philosophy are designed to answer? For there is no one and only theory of knowledge, but an immense variety of rival theories, alike only in that they claim to deal with the same subject matter (and to

1. e.g., p. 60

deal with it better than any of their competitors), although the exact questions which they think it proper to ask when dealing with that subject matter may and do differ from one theory to another. It is, therefore, impossible to avoid controversy over posing the questions; nor could one hope within the limits of this book finally to settle controversy raised. But controversy is desirable; only unreflective prejudice and passive acquiescence are to be avoided.

Since, therefore, a question is to be asked, I put it thus: 'What is present to my mind when I think?' This, it should be said at once, is only a first and very general formulation, which now needs to be whittled down into a more useful shape. What strikes one immediately as unsatisfactory about that formulation is the oddity of supposing that the (or even a) fundamental question about the theory of *knowledge* should be a question about *thinking*. For surely, it will be objected, knowing and thinking are fundamentally different and contrasted intellectual operations; we only say we *think* something is the case when we do not believe that we are entitled to say that we *know* it to be the case. I should ordinarily say, 'I think it's raining', if on looking out of my window, although I could not see any drops falling, I could see people walking about in the street with their umbrellas up. I should not ordinarily say, 'I know it's raining', if that was all the evidence I had to go on; it might, after all, just have stopped raining, but none of the people carrying their umbrellas up had yet noticed it. I should ordinarily say, 'I know it's raining', if on looking out of my window I saw the drops falling or splashing on the road, or if I went outside and felt them on my face and hands. In fact we do not say 'I know . . .' when there is any room for doubt; instead we say 'I think . . .'.

In answer to this objection there are, perhaps, two things to be said. First, 'Theory of Knowledge' is a misnomer. A theory of knowledge is not a theory only about the nature of knowing and the objects of knowledge; if it has any pretensions to completeness, it must be a theory about the range and limits of knowing, and about what happens beyond those limits. As we shall see, most of the problems are set to us precisely because a great many things of which we are in some sense aware and about which we judge are not objects of knowledge at all. Indeed, if all that we were concerned with was our ability to know, then the Theory of Knowledge would be a small and fairly arid field of philosophy; it is precisely our ability for not knowing and our capacity for making mistakes that produce the exciting problems. Therefore, until explained, 'Theory of Knowledge' is a misleading name for the subject, but once explained it should no longer mislead; and as it is the most commonly accepted name I shall continue to use it, employing also 'epistemology' as an exact synonym.

Secondly, in asking the question, 'What is present to my mind when I think?' I was using the word 'think' in the widest possible sense. One of the first lessons one must learn in philosophy is to appreciate that one word does not always have one and only one meaning. A great many disputes both in philosophy and in other subjects, whether theoretical or practical, owe their existence to the fact that the disputants are using the same word (i.e. the same sound if they are talking, or the same marks on paper if they are writing) with undisclosed differences of meaning.

Now, 'think' is used in a variety of senses: e.g. as synonymous with 'believe' or 'judge', as in 'I think we are out of bread'; as synonymous with 'reflect', as 'I have been thinking what to do with my savings'; and again in a much more general sense, as when one asks a companion. 'What are you thinking?' His reply may consist of telling you of something he was remembering, or something he was imagining, or something he was wondering about, and so on. We should not suppose that the only correct answer for him to give to our question, 'What are you thinking?' would be 'Nothing', unless he could truthfully say that he was *thinking that* something was the case (e.g. that we are out of bread), or that he was *thinking about* something, in the sense that he was trying to work out the answer to some problem, whether of practice or of theory. He might well have been doing neither of these things, and yet he could not truthfully answer 'Nothing' to our question, as long as he was conscious at all. True, one often is inclined to answer 'Nothing' when asked what one is thinking. But it is not a strictly truthful answer; and that is often indicated by the answer taking the lamer form of 'Nothing really'.

A man tends to say that he was thinking of nothing either because he was not thinking in either of the two senses mentioned above, or because, apart from the fact that he was not thinking in either of those senses, he prefers not to tell the other person what was going on in his mind. It is less trouble to answer 'Nothing' than to try to describe thoughts which may not be interesting enough to be worth describing, or which may be of such a sort that one would prefer the other person not to know that one was having them. But as long as a man is aware of anything going on in his mind, even if it is only an incoherent stream of ideas or images, then he cannot answer truthfully 'Nothing' to the question, 'What are you thinking?' That is, in this sense, a man is thinking whenever he is conscious of anything, whether his consciousness takes the determinate forms of asserting, denying, questioning, doubting, remembering, imagining, daydreaming, etc., in short, whenever his mind is not a blank. Whether Descartes was right in maintaining that strictly one's mind can never be a blank, or whether the old man was right who said that sometimes he sat and thought and sometimes he just sat, need not concern us here. What nobody is likely to deny is that for most of us most of the time when we are not asleep some stream of consciousness goes on; there is most of the time something 'in' our minds. Therefore the original question, 'What is present to my mind when I think?' can now be seen to be asking what are the objects of consciousness, using consciousness in its widest sense.

It must not, however, be assumed that what we are looking for is a special class of objects called 'objects of consciousness'. Many philosophers in the past have made just that mistake, which is easy to make and important to avoid. There may be a special class of things which are objects of consciousness and not anything else, but so far as we have gone we have no reason for thinking that there is. Again, because different forms of consciousness might well have different objects, we cannot afford to start by assuming that they do not. Ordinary language certainly assumes that what I am aware of when I look around me are things of a different sort from what I am aware of when I am imagining, or, again, when I am dreaming.

Thus we must not at the outset suppose that an object of consciousness is a thing of a special sort; it may be found that things of more than one sort may be objects of different forms of consciousness;

or it may be found that almost anything can be an object of consciousness, if being an object of consciousness simply consists in standing in a certain relation to a mind, just as anybody can be a brother, provided that he is male and that certain biological conditions involving his parents are fulfilled. Being a brother is not being a man of a particular sort or possessing particular characteristics, such as, on the other hand, being bald or pot-bellied is; being a brother is being a man of any sort standing in a particular relationship. So also, being an object of consciousness may be being an object of any sort standing in a particular relationship, namely that of being cognised by a mind.

Because 'thinking' is most commonly understood in one or other of the two senses specified above, i.e. as believing or as reflecting, I propose to substitute for it in its general sense the word 'cognition', which is sufficiently neutral and indeterminate to attract no preconceptions or prejudices. The Theory of Knowledge, then, is that branch of philosophy which has for its study the nature of cognition and its objects.

## 3. *Epistemology and psychology*

A further point which needs clearing up at this stage, at least in a preliminary way, is the relation between Theory of Knowledge and Psychology. Where does the first end and the second begin? and how is one to decide whether a given problem about the mind and its objects calls for a philosophical or a psychological solution? The answer is that no clear-cut answer can be given, that there is, at any rate at present, no absolutely sharp boundary line dividing the two. Just as the other natural sciences attained their independence by splitting off from the amorphous mass of knowledge called 'philosophy' so psychology is at present establishing its independence in the same way.

In England the process began at the end of the seventeenth century with John Locke, whose *Essay Concerning Human Understanding* was a treatise written 'To enquire into the original, certainty, and extent of human Knowledge', and purported to follow 'a historical, plain method'.[1] The subject then known as 'mental philosophy'

1. *Essay*, I, 1, 2.

covered the whole range of questions now brought under the separate headings of theory of knowledge, scientific method, moral philosophy and psychology;[1] and even nowadays for a man to say that he is interested in psychology does not by itself inform his listener what he means; the latter may feel compelled to ask, 'Do you mean philosophical psychology or experimental psychology? Do you sit in your study and introspect? or do you set laboratory puzzles to people and monkeys and rats?'

Nevertheless a distinction can be drawn which is suitable for our purposes. Psychology is an empirical science which tries to discover how our minds work—i.e. what the various mental processes are and what causal laws operate among them—with the object of giving as complete an explanation as possible of mental happenings, both normal and abnormal. Its methods are those of natural science, with the severe handicap that its subject matter is not available for direct inspection (except in the case of the experimenter himself), but has to be inferred from the observed appearances and behaviour of human (or sometimes non-human) bodies. Psychology, then, is interested in causal questions, in finding out *how* minds work. Epistemology, on the other hand, is interested in questions about *what* minds work on, what their material is, what its relation is to objects in the external world, to other persons' minds, to the events of history, and so on.

Clearly, then, a question such as Locke was asking, 'What is the origin of our ideas?' may be a question in genetic psychology, or it may be a question in epistemology; one simply cannot tell without knowing the context to which the question belongs; and again one may find answering the one question an aid towards answering the other. Where they approach each other psychology and the theory of knowledge can only be demarcated by convention; and because in the borderland their interests and methods are similar, no advantage would be gained by insisting on a clear convention, although a time might come later when psychology has developed a higher precision, and when a clear-cut division would be required.

The general distinction between psychology and theory of know-

1. The official title of the longest-standing appointment in psychology in the University of Oxford is 'The Wilde Readership in Mental Philosophy'.

ledge, between the question *how* and the question *what*, may be illustrated by Memory, some of the problems of which will shortly concern us. Suppose that at this minute a memory enters my mind of
myself eating a greasy steak of tunny fish in a village in north Spain
ten years ago. That memory might interest the psychologist in two
ways: he might wonder how events which happened in a man's past,
at a greater or lesser distance in time from the present, should be able
to be recollected as they are in memory; he would be asking a causal
question about how it happens that events from my past can be, as it
were, retained in the file for future reference. He might also wonder
how it is that at that particular minute that particular memory
should occur to me, rather than that some other memory should
occur to me now, or than that particular memory should occur to me
at some other time. Here he would be asking a different causal
question from the first; he would now be asking, given that a causal
account can be given of the availability of my past experiences in
general, what are the conditions of the present situation (my mental
and bodily state, my surroundings, the subject of our conversation,
etc.) which are sufficient to arouse that memory here and now?

The philosopher, on the other hand, has a different but related
interest in memory. What he wants to know is what he is doing when
he is remembering, and in particular he is asking such questions as
these: What is a memory image? What is the relation between the
image present in remembering and the experience remembered? Is
remembering a way of knowing? What criterion is there for distinguishing remembering from imagining? etc. The philosopher may
doubt whether memory gives knowledge about the past, and will
then try to resolve his doubt one way or the other. The psychologist
is not interested in that question; he is concerned with remembering
as a natural event calling for a causal explanation, not with remembering as something which may be direct knowledge of the past or
may be a totally irrational belief about the past. Incidentally, as we
shall see, the case of memory illustrates not only the distinction between psychology and the theory of knowledge, but also their borderland community; for in order to answer some of his questions the philosopher must answer the first of the psychologist's two questions—
that about the availability of past experiences for future memories.

## 4. Two preliminary questions

We may now turn towards indicating some of the problems of epistemology by asking two questions, noting the answers which one would as a normal and not philosophically reflective person be inclined to give, and then considering where these answers lead us. The two questions are:

1. What are we aware of in sense perception?
2. What are we aware of in knowing or believing?

I shall discuss each of these in turn.

## 5. What are we aware of in sense perception?

The plain man's answer to that question might very well be that he was aware of physical objects. He might, if he were a rather astute plain man, add the qualification that physical objects were the things that he was normally aware of, but that there were exceptional cases. For instance, he might say that what he saw when he looked across the room at his wife was a physical object, but that what he saw when he looked at his wife's reflection in a mirror was not a physical object (although the mirror itself was as much a physical object as his wife was). He might hesitate, too, about shadows, and about heat hazes and the illusions which they produce. But, save for exceptions such as these, he would be inclined to say that what he was aware of in sense perception was a physical object. (Most of us, not being blind, tend to think about questions of perception in terms of visual perception, because sight is the most commonly used of our senses. No great harm is done by this, as long as one does not make the mistake of supposing that everything that is true of sight must be true of any of the other senses, or *vice versa*.)

If he were asked to specify further what he was aware of in sense perception, he would probably, rather than attempt a definition of a physical object, give examples, and would say that physical objects were things like tables and chairs, flowers, elephants, typewriters, and so on; in fact, any of the things which he saw when he looked around him, apart from the exceptions mentioned above, were physical objects. And if asked whether he ever saw a table or chair when he looked around him he would, if he thought the question worth answering at all, reply that he did.

Suppose now that we press him to still further specification. Suppose we now put in front of him an ordinary card table and ask him to describe what he sees. He might reply that he sees a card table with a square top covered in green baize, its sides measuring about 3 ft each, with four straight wooden legs, the colour of all the wood-work being dark brown. Asked if he was sure that that was what he saw, he would reply that it was. And, of course, unless we were playing some practical joke on him, he would, in a quite ordinary sense, be right. That *is* what he sees—a card table with a square top, etc. But seeing is not quite as simple and straightforward a matter as one is, as a plain man, liable to assume. It is not merely a case of keeping one's eyes open and one's attention alert, so as to see everything as it really is. Seeing involves among other things interpretation, in the light of one's past experience, of the appearance that is given.

Such interpretation may be inferential, or it may be taking for granted, but it none the less depends on one's experience. For instance, that the table is a card table is not a fact which is literally given to the senses. One recognises it as a card table because its shape and size and its baize-covered top correspond with other tables which one has previously seen used for playing cards. Normally, of course, with fairly familiar objects a man does not have to go through any conscious process of argument in his interpretation of the appearance. He does not need to say to himself: 'There is a table with a square baize-covered top; other tables which I have seen in the past similar in shape, size, and material have been card tables; therefore this is a card table.' Recognition becomes a matter of habit; and life being as short and as busy as it is, it is fortunate that it does. With less familiar objects inference will be required. A mechanical engineer, for instance, faced with a machine of a kind which he has never seen before, may be able by study of its parts and connections to work out what machine it is, and what function it performs.

Again, what a man sees—in the sense of how he interprets the appearance—will depend partly on his interests. A card sharper or a bridge fiend will see our table as a card table, but are unlikely to notice the shape of the legs or the exact colour of the baize top. A carpenter would remark the legs, the jointing of the sides, the variety of the wood, without perhaps noticing that it was a *card* table at all.

A drapery assistant might notice the precise colour, nap, and quality of the baize, and the moth holes in one corner. All would see it as a table, but each would see it to a smaller or greater degree differently from the others.

Let us now ask our subject to tell us the shape of the table top. His answer, naturally, will be that it is square; and if asked why he thinks it is square, he will reply that he thinks so because it looks square. Now, does it look square? It may, in the sense that one judges or assumes that the appearance given to one's sight is the appearance of a square table. But does the actual appearance itself look square? Of course, it almost never does. It only looks square when one's line of vision is exactly or almost exactly at right-angles to the top of the table, which only occurs either if one is suspended above the table or if the table is tilted towards one. In fact, with the table standing on its four legs in the centre of the room, its top presents a prodigious variety of four-sided shapes with opposite pairs of sides more or less parallel, as the observer views it from different angles and distances. If there are two observers, and if they are standing anywhere but very close indeed to each other, the same table will simultaneously present different appearances to each of them.

Nor is it any peculiarity of shape only about our protean table. Its size will look different according to the distance of the observer from it, and to the nature of the medium through which he sees it: we all know how an object 'looms large' when it is indistinctly seen through a fog or a room filled with smoke. The colour of the baize or the woodwork will look different in varying lights, seen through varying mediums (including the shading of the observer's sunglasses if he is wearing them), or seen under different physiological conditions of the observer's own body; jaundice gives things a yellowish tinge, and the taking of drugs such as santonin will play queer tricks with colours.

## 6. Distinction between sensing and perceiving

These considerations suggest that some distinction may have to be drawn between what we are immediately aware of in sense experience (the greenish parallelogram-shaped figure) and what we claim to perceive (the square baize-covered top of a card table). They could be supported by others: it can hardly be doubted that the advanced drunkard sees his pink rats, nor equally that the rats are not there; squinting or pressing one eyeball produces double vision, but they are hardly supposed to produce a second real card table confusedly overlapping with or merging into the first; a man mistakenly hailing another in the street as his friend Jones whom he has not seen for years, when in fact the other is a total stranger called Brown, is having an illusion as much as the traveller in the desert who sees an oasis but discovers it to be a mirage.

Further examples, which suggest the need for distinction between what is given in sense experience and what we take the given to be, could be multiplied, but one more must suffice. At school a boy early learns that the stars are at such an enormous distance from the earth that despite the great speed of light the appearance which he sees when he looks at, say, the Pole Star one night, is the appearance of the Pole Star not as it is at the time of seeing it, but as it was some four hundred years before. Few of us, at the age at which we first acquire the information, are sufficiently inquisitive to ask what the relation then must be between what we are immediately aware of as we look up into the sky and the Pole Star itself. If we were, we should realise that it would be difficult to claim that what we were aware of literally *was* the Pole Star. For if the Pole Star were suddenly to be extinguished now, its extinction could not be noticed by us until over four hundred years had elapsed.

Fortunately, most of the distances at which we observe the objects that chiefly preoccupy our attention (unless we happen to be astronomers) are so small that the passage of light from them to us is for practical purposes instantaneous; in principle the complication remains, but because it makes no discernible difference we ignore it; in fact, the vast majority of mankind does not even reach the stage of ignoring it, but remains in the earlier untroubled state of total ignorance about it.

Distinctions such as the above, between what a man senses and what he perceives, are not new. Plato called attention to them clearly enough in the fourth century BC,[1] and modern philosophers from

1. e.g. in the *Theaetetus*.

Descartes onwards have devoted much, and some of them most, of
their attention to them. In one form or another some dualist account
has been most commonly offered. Locke held that what we are
immediately aware of in sense experience are 'ideas', which are
wholly mind-dependent but represent the objects of the external
world,[1] and which may be divided into those idea which not only
represent but also resemble their objects, and those ideas which
represent but do not resemble their objects.[2] Berkeley agreed that
the immediate objects of sense experience are 'ideas', but disagreed
about the relation between the ideas and the material objects to
which they belonged. For Locke the relation was something like that
of a map to the territory of which it was the map; for Berkeley the
relation was that of a member of a family to the family itself. A
family is nothing over and above its related members, and a material
object is nothing over and above its component related ideas.[3]
Immediately after Berkeley came Hume who, using slightly different
terminology from his predecessors—what they had called ideas he
preferred to speak of as impressions[4]—adopted an uneasy compro-
mise between Berkeley's opinion[5] and an even more extreme view
according to which our thinking in terms of material objects at all
instead of in terms of discrete, successive impressions, is simply a
mistake we are all guilty, due to our uncritical reliance on imagination.[6]

In more recent days philosophers have tended to change their
language again. Because it would not accord with our normal
present-day use of language to say that when we look at a table we
have 'an idea of it'—indeed, we prefer to reserve that phrase for the
occasions when we think of the table in absence (e.g. when we try to
remember or imagine it)—they commonly distinguish between a
sense datum and its object. 'Sense datum' is a term first used, I

1. *Essay*, II, 1.
2. ib. II, 8, 15.
3. 'A certain colour, taste, smell, figure, and consistence having been observed
to go together, are accounted one distinct thing, signified by the name *apple*.'
*Principles of Human Knowledge*, I, 1. cf. I. 8 and 9.
4. *Treatise of Human Nature*, I, 1, 1.
5. ib. I, 4, 3.
6. *Treatise of Human Nature*, I, 4, 2 and 6.

think, by Bertrand Russell, and has already acquired a vast literature
of its own. Nowadays the philosopher has to make up his mind
between a bewildering variety of theories of perception, almost all
of which centre round the old problem of the relation between the
sense datum (they may prefer some other synonym such as 'sensum',
'visual prehensum', etc.) and its object. Almost all agree that a sense
datum cannot *always* be identified with part of the material object
to which it belongs, and that it is questionable whether one is *ever*
justified in so identifying it.[1]

A rival view argues, I think with some, if not total, justification,
that philosophers have tied themselves in unnecessary knots over
perception by talking of sense data as if they were queer substantial
entities which somehow or other have to be related to other entities
called material objects, and that the question whether there are
sense data or not is an unreal one. Whether one chooses to describe
perceptual experience in terms of sense data is a matter of linguistic
convenience; the sense datum language solves no problems and
creates no new ones.[2]

To pursue any further the complications of sensing and perceiving
belongs to a book specially devoted to the subject of perception,
which this is not. Enough, it is hoped, has been said to suggest that
the answer to the question, 'What are we aware of in sense perception?' is not as straightforward as unreflective common sense supposes, that a distinction needs to be made between the appearance
given to the senses and whatever object it is to which the appearance
belongs. A *prima facie* case exists for dualism, for the view that sense
data, or what we are directly aware of, are in some way intermediate
between our minds and material objects. Just what the relation of
mediation is, or even whether it is in all situations the same, does not
here concern us. Consequently I use the term 'sense datum' to mean
'Whatever I am directly aware of in sensation,' leaving open the
question whether sense data are ever or always substantives separate
from the objects to which they belong. At least it seems clear

    1. From a very wide range of writings on this subject the following might be
mentioned: H. H. Price, *Perception*; C. D. Broad, *Mind and its Place in Nature*,
ch. IV; G. E. Moore, *Philosophical Studies*, ch. II, V, VII.
    2. cf. A. J. Ayer, *Foundations of Empirical Knowledge*, ch. I.

that one cannot identify all one's sense data, or even all one's normal sense data, with parts of material objects in the way in which we are as non-philosophers unquestioningly prone to identify them.

## 7. What are we aware of in knowing or believing?

This was the second of the two questions I mentioned above. We shall find that the answers to it tend to lead us in a similar direction to that already taken by the answers to the first. The question may be put thus: whenever we know or believe there is something which we know or believe. There is no such thing as just knowing or just believing. They are states of mind which must have objects or accusatives. What, then, are their accusatives? Again, we have no right to suppose initially that they are all of the same kind; and investigation will suggest strongly that they are not.

## 8. Objects of knowledge

Take knowing first, and consider what accusatives we should be inclined to claim for it. There seem to be at least two different kinds of knowing, with correspondingly different objects.

(i) I may say that 'I know Williams' or that 'I know Lords', meaning that I am *acquainted* with them. Knowing, in the sense of acquaintance, would ordinarily be said to have for its accusatives persons and things. Among things places may be the most commonly used accusatives of knowing, but they are not the only ones. The accusative may be an animal, such as a dog: a man asked if he knows Robinson's dog might reply that he does (or that he does not); he would not ordinarily reply that he did not understand the question. Or it may be an inanimate object: a man might say that he knew Brown's old car, but had not yet seen his new one. Now, to say that persons and things are the accusatives of knowing, in the sense of acquaintance, is certainly not the whole story. In the first place it would need further explanation, to make clear exactly what acquaintance is, and under what conditions we may claim to be acquainted with a person or a thing; we habitually talk as if acquaintance were not a simple relation, but a complex relation subject to modifications or to variations in degree. We speak of 'having met Williams once or twice, but not really knowing him', of 'just knowing him, but that is all', of 'knowing Lord's slightly but knowing Old Trafford much better', and so on. Secondly, if Bertrand Russell is right, it is not correct to say that persons and things are the accusatives of acquaintance; for all that we are actually acquainted with are (a) the particular appearances of persons and things given in sense experience, and (b) the relations which do or may hold between them.[1] However, neither of these qualifications need here concern us. For our purposes it will be sufficient to say that there is a sort of knowing which is acquaintance, and which has for its accusatives persons and things; that both the relation and the accusative may turn out to be much less straightforward does not matter here.

(ii) I may say that 'I know that Williams is away' or that 'I know that the match at Lord's is over', meaning not that I am acquainted with either Williams or Lord's, but that I know something about them. What characterises knowledge in this sense is that one knows *that* something is the case. The accusative here is not a person or a thing, but a fact about them. And although I may very often be acquainted with the person or thing about whom or which I am claiming to know a fact, it is not necessary that I should be. We should not ordinarily say that it was necessary to know Mr Attlee in order to know that he was Labour MP for Limehouse, that he first became Prime Minister in 1945, that he succeeded Mr Winston Churchill in the occupancy of 10 Downing Street, etc. That is to say, one can have knowledge in sense (ii) without knowing in sense (i). But the reverse is not the case. I cannot know Mr Attlee without knowing any facts about him. I might know very few: I might, for instance, be totally ignorant of his political career; I might not even know his name; but at least I should know what he looked like. It would not be sense to say that I knew Mr Attlee but knew absolutely nothing about him.

But although these two ways of knowing are related they are fundamentally different. It is unfortunate that in English the same word is commonly used for both, for this tends to obscure their difference; other languages are better equipped, e.g. French ('*connaître*' and '*savoir*'), German ('*kennen*' and '*wissen*'), Italian ('*conos-*

1. *Problems of Philosophy*, ch, v; *Mysticism and Logic*, ch. x.

*cere*' and '*sapere*'). In the case of the second member of each pair the accusative is a fact, which may be singular, having a specific date and place (e.g. 'I am now in the middle of Trafalgar Square'), or it may be universal, having no specific location in either time or space (e.g. 'If $x$ is greater than $y$, and $y$ is greater than $z$, then $x$ is greater than $z$'). The difference between knowing (acquaintance) and knowing (knowledge that) is so great that some philosophers have been led into asserting that acquaintance is not a form of knowing at all. Such an assertion is perhaps typical of the confusion into which one can be drawn by uncritical subservience to words, and by supposing that one word must be the name for one and only one thing, or for things of only one sort.

The statement that acquaintance is not a form of knowing is both harmless and true if what it means is that acquaintance is different from knowing that. But if the maker of such a statement then goes on to say, as he usually does, that therefore the word 'know' is incorrectly applied to cases of acquaintance, he is making a quite unwarrantable assertion. The word 'know' is correctly so applied, if when it is so applied it is understood in the sense in which it is intended. What this comes to is that there are at least two senses of the word 'know', and that the philosopher who says that one of these senses (acquaintance) is wrong is simply muddled.

## 9. Objects of belief

Turning now from knowing to believing and asking what the latter has for its accusatives, we find some important but hardly surprising differences. In the first place there is no belief corresponding to acquaintance; belief is always belief *that*. Certainly we do talk of believing a person, but there we mean that we believe that what he says is true. Again, it is common enough to speak of believing in a person or in a thing (e.g. a policy of action or a religious doctrine), as when a man says 'I don't believe in the five-day week.' Here what is meant is that he holds or rejects a certain belief *that*; our man does not believe that the five-day week is in the best interest of the country. He may have reasons which are claimed to justify his belief, or he may hold that his belief goes beyond reasons, and in such a case he may prefer to speak of 'faith' than of 'belief'. But in all cases he is believing that something is so; and therefore, if belief in any way corresponds to knowledge, it will have to correspond to it in its second sense, that of knowledge that, the sense in which knowing has for its accusative a fact.

Can we then say that belief has for its accusative a fact? Clearly we cannot, for what a man believes very often is not a fact. It is not a fact that the earth's surface is flat, or that the Second World War ended in 1944, or that water contracts when it freezes. But although none of the above is a fact, there is no difficulty in imagining somebody believing it. Until a certain date in the world's history, almost everybody believed the first; and no doubt, from time to time, some man will mistakenly believe the second or the third. What, indeed, chiefly distinguishes belief from knowledge is that while the latter cannot the former can be false; and no epistemological theory can claim to be adequate which does not account for false as well as for true belief. Whatever may be the case with true belief, false belief cannot have facts for its accusatives, and must therefore have something else. Before asking what this something else must be, we should turn to consider briefly true belief, and to ask what it has for its accusatives. It has been maintained for a variety of reasons, of which I shall mention four, that it too cannot have facts for its accusatives.

The first argument states that it cannot be a fact that the mind has before it in true belief because, if it were, there would be nothing to distinguish true belief from knowledge; and yet we clearly do find it necessary to distinguish them. One man may know what another believes, e.g. one may know that it is raining because he has just come in from outside, and the other truly believe it because the first has come in with his mackintosh wet; or a man may first truly believe and then know the same thing. Now without disputing this need to distinguish true belief from knowledge I do not think the argument at all sound as it stands. For, first, knowledge and true belief might be different even though their objects were the same, because the relation of knowing was different from the relation of believing; and, secondly, it might be possible to be aware of a fact and yet not to recognise that it was a fact, just as one can meet an American and yet fail to recognise him as an American. Nevertheless the argument does carry some weight: whether the object of a true belief is actually a fact or not, it certainly is not recognised as one; for then one would know that one's belief was true; but no belief can be known (by the same person and at the time of holding the belief) to be true, for that would make it not true belief but knowledge. Whether or not, then, the object of a true belief is in a certain context to be called a fact, it is hardly to be so called in its context of accusative to the belief.

The second and third arguments raise difficulties about time, the future and the past. I can have true beliefs about the future—e.g. my present belief that it will rain some time tomorrow will be true, if it does rain some time tomorrow. But, it is said, how can I have the fact of it raining tomorrow before my mind now? I cannot possibly have it, for it is not a fact at all until it does rain, which is not going to happen until tomorrow. Similarly I can have true beliefs about the past—e.g. that Queen Victoria was on the English throne in 1886. But I cannot have the fact before my mind as the accusative of my belief, because that fact is over and done with, and belongs to the past of eighty years ago. In addition there is the further difficulty that in 1886 I had not been born; how could I have as the object of a present believing a fact which ante-dated my own birth by a number of years? Both these arguments are, I think, invalid, because they confuse facts with events. Events occur in time and have dates, but facts do not. I have deliberately refrained from attempting a definition of a fact, in order not to raise too many complicated questions at once. But I have been trying to use the word 'fact' in a sense which would be readily accepted by the reader as the sense in which he uses it as an ordinary man, whatever view he may eventually find himself driven to as a philosopher. If events have temporal locations, but facts do not, then it is sense to say of an event that it has not yet happened or that it occurred eighty years ago, but it is not sense to say the same thing of a fact.

The fourth argument for the view that true beliefs do not have facts as their objects is that the object of a true belief must be of the same sort as the object of a false belief, the difference between them being the difference of relation between the objects and what makes the belief true in the one case and false in the other. It is said that truth is a correspondence between the object of a belief and fact, and that falsity is the non-correspondence of belief to fact. This is obviously an attractive view: it has the merit of being tidy, of neatly indicating both what is common to true and false belief (their objects) and what distinguishes one from the other (the difference of their relation to fact), and of according with what we commonly say on the subject in everyday life. We do speak of a man's beliefs conforming with, or running violently counter to, the facts, of the facts agreeing with what he has said, or of their contradicting him, of comparing his opinion with the facts, of confronting him with the facts, and so on. All these may be ways of saying that there is a relation of correspondence between a true belief and the facts, and a relation of non-correspondence between a false belief and the facts. Nevertheless, despite its attractions this view, as we shall see later, has its disadvantages which make it hard to accept, at least in any straightforward way. But if it can be replaced by another account of truth which preserves its merits—treating true belief *qua* belief as on all fours with false belief—so much the better.

We have seen now that false beliefs clearly cannot have facts as their accusatives, and that although most of the arguments for the view that true beliefs cannot have them either do not stand up to investigation, yet there would be an advantage if both could be treated alike; and further that the first argument does seem to make it extremely difficult to maintain that the object of a true belief is simply a fact; it does at least look to be something else as well, if we are to avoid the conclusion that there is no such thing as true belief.

The similarity between the position which we find ourselves in as a result of considering the question, 'What are we aware of in knowing and believing?' and the position to which we were led over the earlier question, 'What are we aware of in sense perception?' may now be becoming clearer. There we saw that it is necessary to distinguish between the appearances or sense data actually prehended by a man in sense experience and the material objects to which they belong; now we see that in the case of belief it is necessary to distinguish certainly between what a man believes and what makes his belief false, and possibly also between what he believes and what makes his belief true. Required to use some name for the object of a man's belief, philosophers commonly use the word 'proposition'; what I believe is a proposition, and my belief is true if the proposition corresponds with the facts, false if it does not. Again, a proposition is normally distinguished from a sentence by saying that a sentence is a form of words combined according to the grammatical and syntactical rules of the language to which the sentence belongs, while a proposition is not a form of words at all, but is what the sentence means.

For instance, 'I think, therefore I am' is a different sentence from 'I am conscious, therefore I exist', for the words are different both in shape when written and in sound when spoken; but the proposition expressed by each sentence is the same, for both have the same meaning. Again, 'I think, therefore I am,' 'Cogito ergo sum', 'Je pense, donc je suis' are three different sentences, each belonging to a different language, but all three express the same proposition; what Descartes meant when he asserted 'Cogito ergo sum' is the same as what he meant when he translated it into 'Je pense, donc je suis', and the same as what an Englishman means if he translates it into 'I think, therefore I am.' We are therefore asked to make a threefold distinction between sentences, propositions, and facts. Only the distinction between the last two need concern us in this book.

## 10. The difficulties of dualism

The brief discussion first of sense experience and then of judgment does *prima facie* suggest that our original epistemological question, 'What is the mind aware of in cognition?' must be answered by some form of dualism, i.e. that perceiving and believing are not straightforward acts or states of consciousness which directly apprehend material objects and facts, but that they apprehend them, if they apprehend them at all, indirectly via the mediation of sense data and propositions; sense data and propositions will then represent their objects and facts, and in the case of error will misrepresent them. What, then, is the need for further discussion? Having found that perception and belief are more involved than we ordinarily suppose, we seem driven into acceptance of epistemological dualism; the two cases are alike in that respect, although they are unlike in that their objects both mediate and immediate are different, and they may further be unlike in that the relation in each case between representative object and represented object may be different. However, the dualism required in each case is simple and intelligible. Are we then to accept it and leave the matter there? Unfortunately we cannot. The objections to a dualist position are at least as disastrous as the difficulties which tempt one into it. They can be illustrated most simply by applying them to Locke's theory of sense perception, which by its very clarity most openly exposes itself to them; to everyone who has studied Locke in even the most elementary way they will be, of course, familiar.

According to the theory, we never perceive the objects in the external world directly, but only mediately via interposed data, which Locke calls ideas, although, as we have seen,[1] 'idea' is probably a misleading word to use for the same purpose nowadays, because we tend to use it in a different and more restricted sense than Locke's. What we actually and literally see, that is, what presents itself to our sight as we look around us, is not, as we might ingenuously suppose, an external world populated by objects that have an existence quite apart from their being perceived, that continue to exist when not being perceived, and that may in general behave in a manner quite outside the percipient's control. It is, of course, true that such a world exists, but I, as a percipient, never come into direct contact with it. What I do come into direct contact with are its effects, which are the 'ideas' I have when I look around, the data of my sense experience. These data represent to me the real external objects which cause them, and they, as it were, provide me with a picture of the real world beyond.[2]

In some respects this picture is bound to be inaccurate, because some of my data are not at all like the objects or characteristics of objects which they represent. Colour for instance is in this way inaccurate, because the objects of the real world are not coloured at all, but produce the appearances of colour by 'the different degrees and modifications of their motions.' That is, all that there really is behind the appearances of colour is a vibration or agitation of the

1. See p. 21.
2. Since this book was written I have come to have serious doubts about the interpretation of Locke given here. See my edition of his *Essay* (Collins, Fontana Library, 1964).

elements or atoms of external objects; these vibrations cause us, when we look, to see colours of determinate shades and intensities, but if we suppose that the colours are like the qualities which produce them and which they represent, we shall be making a mistake of the same sort as if we suppose that the symbol for a church on the map resembles the actual church on the ground which it represents. In like case with colours are 'tastes and sounds, and other the like sensible qualities; which, whatever reality we by mistake attribute to them, are in truth nothing in the objects themselves, but powers to produce various sensations in us'.[1] Contrasted with them are those qualities of objects which are represented by ideas which do resemble them, and which are 'bulk, figure, texture, and motion'.

Locke's theory therefore may be summarised as follows:

(a) What is immediately given in sense perception is never the whole nor even a part of an external object; it is instead something which is caused by the object and which represents it.

(b) Of these immediate representative data some are like the qualities they represent, others are not.

Now such a theory of sense perception might conceivably be possible, for, so far as I can discover, it does not contain any internal self-contradictions. But it does suffer from the grave disadvantage that if it is true Locke (or anybody else) is by its very truth precluded from ever knowing, or even having the slightest reason for supposing, that it is true; and therefore none of the arguments which Locke advances in its favour could be available for him. He is therefore faced with the dilemma: if the arguments for the theory are available to him, the theory cannot be true; if the theory is true, no reasons can be available for accepting it. Neither of these is a horn which reason can comfortably embrace. They can be briefly explained by considering in turn each of the two propositions (a) and (b) above, in which they are summarised.

(a) What is immediately given is not an object or part of it; it is something caused by the object and representative of it. Now, how does one recognise anything to be a representative of something else? Either one can find out for oneself by comparing representative and represented—as when having seen an original picture, say in

1. *Essay*, II, 8, 14.

the Louvre, one then sees a reproduction hanging on the wall of a picture dealer's shop; or one can be shown some title which the representative carries on itself, guaranteeing that it does represent what it purports to represent—as when the inspector coming to read the electric meter produces the company's card certifying that he is their inspector. Which of these alternatives is open to Locke? The second is not, for not only do the data of sense experience not carry any certificate of authenticity, guaranteeing that they do represent what they claim to represent, but they do not even claim to represent anything at all. Considered barely as the data of sensation they make no representative claim of any kind. If any such claim is made at all, it is made on their behalf—but by whom? or by what? In themselves they display no feature which suggests that there is something else beyond which they represent, and taken at their face value they are simply what they seem to be, the colours, shapes, and noises presented to sense. If we take them at more than their face value and suppose them to represent something else, that is because of some interpretation which we put upon them, not because of any characteristic or mark which we discover in the data themselves.

Similarly, the first method of identifying a representative is not open to Locke. We cannot compare ideas with objects so as to discern the relation of representative or copy and original which holds between them, for the simple reason that according to Locke's principle which we are now considering we are never aware of the original except via the mediation of the representative. But, if that is so, we should never have any reason for supposing that there was anything beyond, let alone that it was related to our datum as original to representative. One cannot, merely by inspecting a hand-painted picture, tell or have any reason for telling that it is or that it is not a copy. The information provided simply by the picture itself is no evidence either way; it only becomes evident when it is combined with further information, such as that the signature is that of an artist who is independently known to specialise in copying, and so on, the simplest and clearest evidence of all being to have seen the original picture from which ours was copied.

Again, one just cannot tell from the mere seeing of a film whether it is 'based on an original story by X' or not; to tell that, one needs to have read the story, or to have heard from somebody else whom one has reason to regard as truthful that it is based on an original story, or to recognise in the film certain qualities which it shares with other films which are *independently* known to be taken from some original story. But, if Locke's account of perception is correct, we are precisely in the position of men in the cinema who are constantly relating the films which they see to 'original stories', but who have no reason whatever for even suspecting that there are such things as original stories. As long as our experience is confined to what is representative, we can have no reason for supposing that it *is* representative; only when we can step outside the circle of representative objects into the outer circle of represented objects does the relation of representative to original become verifiable or even significant; but it is precisely this step that, if Locke's basic epistemological principle is true, we can never take.

(*b*) Locke also claimed to distinguish between those data which do resemble their objects and those which do not. Little need be said about this claim, for if the objections above are sound then *a fortiori* the present claim must fall. Now, we are in the position of men faced with a painting, possessed of no other relevant information at all, and asked not only whether it is a copy but also whether it is a good or a bad copy, and again in precisely what features it is good and in which bad. How could one possibly say? To tell whether a copy is good or not I must be able to compare copy with original, either this copy with its original, or this copy with other copies and those with their originals. If at every point I am prevented from comparing copy with original, then I can never have any reason for supposing that it is a good or a bad copy, let alone for indicating in which respects it is good or bad.

Summarising, then, we may say that Locke's epistemological dualism leads logically to the conclusion that, if his theory of perception is true, we can have no reason for supposing that the data of sense experience are representative, that some resemble their objects and some do not, or for distinguishing which do and which do not, or for indicating the respects in which the resemblances do and do not hold. The veil of sense has become an iron curtain with a vengeance.

B

We have illustrated the difficulties of a naïve dualism by Locke's theory of perception. In his theory of belief similar difficulties crop up over the relations between propositions and facts which, as this book is not about Locke, need not concern us here. The conclusion to which we seem to be driven is that dualism, at any rate in the crude form in which it was advocated by Locke, will not work. If any form of dualism is to be acceptable at all, it will have to be less simple than that which we have so far considered; and if a distinction is to be made between the immediate data of cognition, on the one hand, and material objects or facts, on the other, the relation between them will have to be less straightforward than the relation between images in a mirror and the originals which they accurately or distortedly reflect. On the other hand, our initial difficulties suggest that some account not totally removed from dualism is required: it seemed over-ingenuous to suppose that what we directly *see* are material objects, or that what we *believe* are facts. In order to look for a way out of the present uncomfortable impasse, in which dualism is apparently found to be both necessary and untenable, I propose to turn to consider the particular case of memory. The difficulties in the way of providing a wholly satisfactory account of memory bring out clearly the *prima facie* attractions both of a dualist and of a non-dualist theory of knowledge.

# 2

## MEMORY

### 1. Different kinds of memory

We have already seen some of the dangers of supposing that a word has the same meaning on all occasions and in every context. They crop up again in the case of 'memory' and 'remembering', both of which are used to refer to situations of different kinds. One may be tempted to say that the words are correctly used only when applied to situations of one kind, that that is the only *true* memory, and that other uses are to a greater or lesser degree misuses; but it would be a mistake to succumb to the temptation and to say, for instance, that one proposed to discuss real memory, not the other 'so-called' sorts of memory. I propose to discuss only one sort of memory, which is such that there are important differences between it and other sorts of memory; but the fact that for our purposes only one sort of memory is interesting does not entitle us to say that the other sorts are not really memory at all.

We commonly speak of remembering how to do something—to ride a bicycle, to hold a rifle, or to swim. This remembering how does not (or need not) involve any act of thinking at all, but consists in still possessing the ability to perform the activity in question. I show you that I still remember how to ride a bicycle simply by mounting the bicycle and riding it. Another sort of remembering how does involve an act of thought, as when I have to work something out: remembering how to do Pythagoras' theorem consists in being able to work out (by thinking) the stages of the deduction which lead to the desired conclusion. Again we speak of remembering a poem, or of remembering the dates of the kings of England—meaning that we can recite the poem now if asked, or that we can run through the catalogue of dates if necessary. All the above cases are legitimate uses of 'memory' or 'remember'. But there is one quite different use, which need not and usually does not apply to any of the above cases; and that is the sense which matters to us here—the sense in which I remember meeting Jones at Newhaven last Tuesday, or having strawberries for tea one day last week, or reading *Macbeth* for the first time when I was in bed with mumps at the age of thirteen or fourteen. If I remember the 'Tomorrow and tomorrow and tomorrow . . .' soliloquy from *Macbeth*, in the sense of being able to recite it, I may or may not also remember learning it or hearing it declaimed or declaiming it myself. Remembering in the latter sense is not necessary to remembering in the former sense, although sometimes it may be a help (and sometimes not). We would not say that a man did not remember how to ride a bicycle if, although he could still ride one, he could no longer remember where or when or on what machine he first learned to ride; and if he was doubtful whether he could remember how to ride, he would not find his task made easier by recalling memories of his first failures and triumphs in mastery of a bicycle; on the other hand, if he was trying to remember Macbeth's soliloquy and stuck at a word, say at 'creeps in this *something* pace from day to day', he might find it easier to supply the missing word by recalling the gesture the actor made in a particular performance of the play, or the sound of his voice, or the expression on his face at the time.

The important point, however, is that remembering in the sense in which I remember a particular recitation of the soliloquy is extraneous to remembering the soliloquy. We are concerned here only with the first, the sense in which remembering is a cognitive act of the mind which occurs *now* and which has for its object an event or series of events belonging to the *past*; it is not necessary that I should think of the event in question as precisely dated, as belonging to last Wednesday rather than to last Tuesday, or to the morning rather than to the afternoon, but it is necessary that I should think of it as being in some degree or other removed from the present, and of course removed backwards into the past, not forwards into the future. We may contrast this sense of 'memory' with the others, and we may, as I shall for our purposes, ignore the other senses, but we may not say that this is the only true or proper sense.[1] For convenience, and to avoid repeated explanations, I shall in what follows use 'memory' in the one sense only, and should be understood to mean by it that sort of memory the acts of which are cognitive acts directed towards events belonging to the past; we shall be concerned with acts of remembering, rather than with memory as a disposition or a capacity for performing those acts.[2]

## 2. Remembering as an act

What, then, does remembering consist in? More specifically, what is the immediate object of an act of remembering? and if the immediate object is not the same as the object or event remembered, what is the relation between them? As we shall see, various theories of memory have been advanced, all of them anxious to be as little removed as possible, if at all, from the view of common sense. What, then, is the view of common sense, the view which we tend to adopt in our rôle of plain men? The first answer to this question, like the answer to many questions which we as philosophers are inclined to put to ourselves as plain men, is that it is not a question with which the plain man bothers himself; and consequently to attribute to him a definite view on the nature of memory is to represent his outlook as being more clear-cut than it actually is. Nevertheless, he does tend to give an answer, however vague, of one or the other of the two following kinds.

1. The context in which the words 'memory' and 'remember' are used may by itself leave their meaning ambiguous, as for instance when one speaks of remembering a person. Remembering a person's face normally consists in recalling some one or more experiences of seeing it, so that when asked, 'Do you remember him?' that is what is normally meant. But 'Do you remember him?' may instead be asking a remember how question and mean the same as 'Could you pick him out on an identification parade?' Perhaps picking him out requires an act of memory in our cognitive sense, but being able to pick him out and having him as the object of a cognitive memory act are not the same thing.

2. In speaking of *acts* of memory I mean here no more than that events of remembering occur, and am not committed to the view that when I remember I am an *agent*.

He may, on the one hand be a Naïve Realist, i.e. he may hold that what is immediately before his mind when he remembers is the actual event[1] remembered, or at least part of it; that if, for example, in August 1944 he shot at a German soldier in the streets of Florence, and if now he remembers doing that, then what is immediately before his mind now is the very event, or part of it, which occurred then. In so far as ordinary language is a guide to our views, to speak of 'recalling an experience', of 'casting one's mind back into the past', and so on suggests the Naïve Realist view of memory.

On the other hand, the plain man may be a little more sophisticated. He may suspect that the previous view will produce awkward difficulties over time and over errors: how can there now be present to my mind an event which occurred and ended several years ago? how, if the actual past event is now present, can I make the mistakes of misremembering which I certainly do? For these two reasons (both of them, I hope to show, bad reasons) the plain man more usually favours another view, according to which what is immediately before the mind in an act of remembering is an image or a series of images, which somehow or other represent the past event remembered. We tend in fact to a dualist theory of memory, and a dualism at that which is suspiciously like the dualist theory of sense perception which we have already seen to be untenable in the form in which Locke advanced it. Why if we tend to be Naïve Realists in our outlook on perception do we follow an opposite tendency in our outlook on memory, and there favour a dualist view? why do we suppose that remembering is done by having images of the thing or experience remembered? In order to give the answers to these questions clearly it is first necessary to make clear the view in question, always reminding ourselves of the risk of misrepresenting it by the very process of making it clear. But it can, I think, be summarised as follows:

(a) the event remembered is not what is immediately before the mind in remembering;

1. Throughout I talk of memory of *events*. I have confined myself to them simply for the sake of brevity, and should not be taken as suggesting that it would be improper to speak of remembering other things, such as persons or places.

(*b*) what is immediately before the mind in remembering is an image;

(*c*) the image in some way represents or symbolises the events of which it is an image.

The chief reason that induces the ordinary man to believe (*a*) is the temporal reason already given, that the event remembered belongs to the past, is dead and gone, and cannot be part of another event (the remembering) which belongs to the present. The chief reason that induces us to believe (*b*) is not, as we might be tempted to suppose, that we believe that if the event itself is not before the mind then what is before the mind must be an image. The explanation is simpler than that: it is that what we mean in general by 'image' is that an image is the sort of thing that we have before our minds when we remember. This is not offered as a definition of 'image', which for various reasons it cannot be; the whole point is that at the commonsense level we do not work by strict definitions, for examples are easier to produce and will usually serve the purpose just as well. Therefore to say that an image is the sort of thing that we have before our minds when we remember is not to define 'image'; it is instead simply to indicate what one refers to by the word 'image'.

If you come across someone for whom that method of indication will not work, you must try some other way: you may ask him to imagine a monkey tapping on a typewriter, and when he tells you that he is imagining that all right, you tell him that what he now has before his mind is an image. This shows that images are not peculiar to memory (for they occur in imagination too), and *may* not be necessary to it (if the man is speaking the truth when he says that your indication of the meaning of 'image' by means of memory is no help to him); and consequently 'image' cannot be defined in terms of memory. But the fact is that for most people most memories involve images, that *qua* image there is no qualitative difference between a memory-image and an imagination-image; and therefore their reason for holding (*b*) above is quite simply that 'image' is the name for the sort of thing that is (always or often) before the mind in remembering. To ask them what reason we have for calling that sort of thing an image is to ask a nonsensical question. It is as if,

having agreed to call the men drafted under the National Service
Acts 'conscripts', we then asked what reason we had for believing
that they were conscripts.

The reasons for our commonly supposing (c)—that memory-
images in some way represent the events of which they are images—
are again natural enough: to believe (c) is, indeed, the obvious
corollary of believing (a) and (b). I am not saying that any of these
beliefs is correct (or incorrect), but merely that they or something
like them are the beliefs about memory which we as ordinary men,
i.e. in our non-philosophical moments, tend to hold. Now let us
turn to consider them, to determine, if we can, whether they are
correct or not.

### 3. The image theory

The image theory in its simplest form—that remembering consists
in having images which represent the original event—is clearly a
dualist theory, and has received its classical exposition from David
Hume. 'We find by experience, that when any impression has been
present with the mind, it again makes its appearance there as an idea;
and this it may do after two ways: either when in its new appearance
it retains a considerable degree of its first vivacity, and is somewhat
intermediate betwixt an impression and an idea; or when it entirely
loses that vivacity, and is a perfect idea. The faculty, by which we
repeat our impressions in the first manner, is called the MEMORY,
and the other the IMAGINATION.'[1] The data of memory and imagination then are alike in being images (what Hume meant by 'ideas'),
which are reflections of their originals, but differ in that memory-
images possess a vivacity which imagination does not. A further
difference which Hume notes is that memory preserves the order of
the original events, but the imagination need not. If I remember
driving from Oxford to London last week, my memory-images must
present me as travelling in the direction in which I did travel, i.e.
at earlier moments in the journey being nearer to Oxford than at
later moments. But if I am merely imagining an experience, I can as
easily imagine myself travelling from London to Oxford as the other
way round, and I can have an even less orderly series of images than

1. *Treatise of Human Nature*, I, 1, 3.

that: I can dart from one point on the route to another quite regardless of any direction of travel, or whether they are adjacent to each
other; imagination 'is not restrained to the same order and form
with the original impressions; while the memory is in a manner ty'd
down in that respect, without any power of variation'.[1]

Remembering then consists in having images which (i) preserve
the order of the original, the event remembered; and (ii) are marked
by a certain degree of vivacity, less than that of the original experience, but greater than that characterising the images of imagination.
How satisfactory is this account? Does it enable me to determine
that a particular experience is one of remembering rather than of
imagining, with which it is obviously in most danger of being confused? Will Hume's two distinguishing features in fact enable us to
make the distinction?

The first certainly will not, as Hume himself points out:[2] I cannot
tell on *internal* evidence whether a string of images preserves the
order of the original or not; simply by inspecting the images themselves I cannot tell whether the order has been changed or not. In
order to discover that I should have to confront the images with the
original and compare the order in each. But to make this comparison
I should have to be able to remember the original in a direct way,
incompatible with the theory in question; and I should then be in
the absurd position of maintaining *both* that all remembering
consists in having images which represent the original, *and* that to
confirm whether an alleged memory was genuine I should need to
remember by a direct re-acquaintance with the original; it is self-
contradictory to maintain both that all memory is of one sort (i.e.
having images) and that not all memory is of one sort (as it would
not be if re-acquaintance with the past original were possible). Hume
saw this quite clearly and avoided the contradiction by stating that
although (i) above is true—memory-images do preserve their
original order—yet this cannot be used by us as a distinguishing
feature of memory, 'it being impossible to recall the past impressions,
in order to compare them with our present ideas, and see whether
their arrangement be exactly similar'.

1. *Treatise of Human Nature*, I, 1, 3.
2. ib. I, 3, 5.

Consequently Hume finds himself driven back on his second feature contained in (ii), that a memory experience is to be recognised as a memory by the degree of its vivacity: 'it follows that the difference betwixt it [memory] and the imagination lies in its superior force and vivacity. A man may indulge his fancy in feigning any past scene of adventures; nor would there be any possibility of distinguishing this from a remembrance of a like kind, were not the ideas of the imagination fainter and more obscure.'[1] Now Hume involves himself in a number of confusions here which, as we are only incidentally concerned with him, it is not our business to unravel. But if he means by 'vivacity' what he appears to mean, it certainly will not serve as a sufficient mark of memory, and its claim to serve even as a necessary mark is doubtful. Hume nowhere in his text defines 'vivacity', but wherever he explains it he does it on the lines indicated in the above quotation, suggesting that greater vivacity consists in brighter, more vivid, and more precise detail, and that memory-images are less hazy than those of imagination, and so on. Now vivacity, in that sense, certainly will not serve as a sufficient mark of memory, for an image of the prescribed degree (whatever that is) of vivacity does not have any sign of *pastness* about it. Vividness as such is no indication at all that the image stands for some previous experience. That is to say, even if it be true that all remembering does consist in having lively images, that cannot be all that it consists in; for them to be *memory-images* they would have to possess some other feature than their liveliness, and it would be this feature having special reference to the past which would mark them out as images of memory.

In the second place, it is not even true that all memories are lively, or that all memory-images are more lively than any imagination-image. Most of us have had the experience of thinking we remember something which in fact never occurred—we are in fact imagining it. Similarly most of us have had the experience of not being sure whether what we are thinking of actually happened or not—i.e. whether what we are doing now is remembering or imagining. Both of these experiences, of thinking you are remembering when you are only imagining (and *vice versa*), and of not being sure whether you

1. ib.

are remembering or imagining, most readily occur over things which one would very much *like* to have happened, or which one would very much *dislike* to have happened. It is an easy matter for a soldier who wishes that he had performed a certain act of bravery in a battle so to think of himself as having performed it that in the end he may feel sure that he did, or not feel sure whether he did or not; it is too, unfortunately, an easy matter for the introvert who is also something of a coward so to be preyed on by thoughts of his own poor conduct that he ends up by thinking he remembers an act of cowardice which in fact he is only imagining. Hume himself was well enough aware of this, that memory-images can sink in vivacity below those of imagination,[1] but does not seem to have faced the consequence—that vivacity is not only not the sufficient mark of memory, but is not even necessary. He seems to have been misled from believing (what seems to be true) that for most of us most memory-images are more vivid than most imagination-images into believing (what is certainly false) that *the* difference between the two is one of vivacity.

As we have seen, even if it were true, as it is not, that all memory-images were more vivid than those of imagination, that would not be enough by itself to suggest that they were images of *memory*. What is characteristically memory about them is still missing.[2] This indeed is a fundamental difficulty of a straightforward dualist theory of memory, a difficulty which Hume's account well brings out. If to remember is merely to have images of a certain kind, why should we suppose, let alone claim to know, that they refer to the past at all? Before we could use vivacity as a criterion for determining a memory

1. *Treatise of Human Nature*, I, 3, 5.
2. Students of Hume will remember that various passages in the *Treatise* (notably the end of I, 3, 8, and two notes in the Appendix on I, 3, 7) suggest a different interpretation of vivacity from that which I have followed above. In them Hume seems to be trying to say that by 'vivacity' he does not mean intensity or clarity of detail, but instead a property of seeming real, of genuineness or authenticity. While this interpretation would make his general theory of impressions and ideas more plausible than it otherwise is, it gives him no particular advantage in the case of memory; for he would still be up against the difficulty that there is no apparent reason why an authentic-seeming image should be thought of as referring to the past. Memory-images certainly are thought of as referring to the past; and therefore Hume's deficiency on the orthodox interpretation is not remedied by this alternative interpretation.

experience we should have to establish, at any rate inductively, that memory experiences have this vivacity; and to do that we should have to have some other way of distinguishing authentic memory experiences, at least in some cases. But, if to remember is simply to have an image which does in fact represent its original, although we have no means of confirming that it does, what way of distinguishing memory experiences is left to us? The answer is that memory cannot be analysed simply in terms of having images; we need to give some account of the fact that some images seem to have a reference to the past which some others do not, in order to explain our even supposing that some of our experiences are experiences of remembering; and if memory is to be authenticated, i.e. if we are to have any ground for supposing that some memories at least are veridical, we need to have some means of authentication beyond images themselves. A man does not in fact remember by having certain images and by inferring from having them that he must in the past have had the experience which they represent; nor if he did make such an inference would it have any validity.

## 4. The familiarity theory

We pass now to a theory which is like the one we have been discussing, but which does attempt to fill the gap in Hume's account. According to the present theory, which is very clearly expounded by Bertrand Russell in his book called *The Analysis of Mind*,[1] a memory-image is distinguished from others by a feeling of *familiarity* which marks it; and it is this feeling of familiarity, which is at its vaguest the feeling that 'this has happened before somewhere', that provides us with the sense of pastness essential to memory. To remember, then, is (i) to have an image marked by this feeling of familiarity, and (ii) to formulate a belief based on the feeling of familiarity that 'this' belongs to the past, where 'this' refers both to the image and to the event remembered.[2] Russell's insistence on the need to distinguish between the feeling of familiarity, on the one hand, and the belief based on it, on the other, seems due to his desire to allow the feeling to an animal, e.g. a horse returning to its stable, to which he

1. Lecture IX.
2. ib., pp. 179-80.

would deny the ability to believe.[1] It seems to be a highly questionable distinction, and in any case is irrelevant to our purposes, because for a human being part of an experience of feeling a sense of familiarity is surely the belief (it may, of course, not be a strong belief which we would call conviction, but only a very faint one such as we would call suspicion) that 'this has happened before somewhere'. We can therefore ignore the distinction between (i) and (ii) above, and can treat the feeling of familiarity as including an element of belief, however faint and inarticulate the belief may be.

What, then, is there to be said about the theory? First, it seems undeniable that our memory-images do have this recognisable familiarity about them, and that it is that which distinguishes them from other images. It is not, of course, confined to images: we can in sense experience feel that there is something familiar about a face opposite us in the railway carriage, or about a village we are passing through; and we may go on being worried by the feeling until we succeed in placing the face or the village in question, the placing itself being a remembering. When I am taken to a place and asked 'Do you remember this?' I look round for something that strikes me as familiar; if nothing does I have to answer that I do not remember it. Again, it is familiarity which causes the confusion in the cases where I think I remember something, but am wrong because I am only imagining it: the trouble is that in such a case I have imagined it so often before, wishing that it had happened, that the images themselves become familiar, and I forget that I *wish* it had happened (for we more easily forget what we would like to forget), with the consequence that I really believe that I am remembering—or with the alternative consequence that I am genuinely unsure whether I am remembering or not.[2]

1. Lecture IX, p. 169.
2. Although in the text I continue, following usual practice, to use the word 'familiarity', I am not sure that it is a happy word for the feeling characteristic of memory-images. For that feeling seems, in my experience at least, quite different from the feeling I have when I meet somebody and find his face familiar. In the latter case I am not claiming to remember (that I would like to but cannot is what is irritating), and the feeling of familiarity seems to be just the belief (which may range from conviction to suspicion) that this face did occur in a past experience of mine, although I cannot now remember it. A memory-image, on the other hand, is accompanied not by that feeling of familiarity, but by a feeling of right-

## 5. Objections to the theory

One sometimes comes across an objection to this theory, that memory cannot be explained in terms of familiarity, because familiarity presupposes memory. Now, to state the matter like that, that familiarity presupposes memory, disguises the fact that there are two objections here, which need to be kept distinct from each other, and neither of which is valid. The first objection is saying that the notion of memory is at least part of the notion of familiarity, that one cannot explain what one means by saying something is familiar except by saying that one (however vaguely) remembers or seems to remember it; and if the notion of familiarity contains as an essential element the notion of memory, one cannot define memory in terms of familiarity, for if any definition is to be possible at all it will have to be given the other way round, familiarity in terms of memory. Now this objection is surely invalid, because there is surely no reason for supposing that the notion of memory is *part* of the notion of familiarity. What does seem true is that when I say 'This seems familiar' I could have said without any change of meaning 'I seem to remember this'. But as that the two statements are synonymous is precisely what the theory in question is asserting it can hardly be objected to it that it is asserting it. From the fact that for 'I remember this' there can be substituted 'This is familiar' it does not follow that 'I remember this' is *part* of the meaning of 'This is familiar,' that the notion of memory is part of the notion of familiarity. The objection wrongly supposes that it does follow.

The other objection concealed in the statement that familiarity presupposes memory centres round the notion of pastness. Pastness is an admitted element in the notion of familiarity. But if remembering consisted in having images plus a feeling of familiarity, how

ness. I think that the only images which I experience affected by the feeling of familiarity are analogous to seeing the unplaceable face, i.e. those images which I believe I have had before, but I cannot remember when. Of course, faces which I *can* place are familiar, too. But I suspect we mean something different again there by 'familiar'. We do not mean that seeing such faces is accompanied by a belief that we have seen them before somewhere, and that we can place them, for it clearly is not. We mean by saying that the face is familiar that we could, if asked, recognise it or quote memories of it. In fact, if a face is familiar in this sense, we never ordinarily say that it is: one is never struck with the familiarity of one's wife's face.

could we acquire the notion of pastness at all? Must we not have some other more direct cognitive relation to a previous experience, in order to have the notion of pastness? This objection is not, like the first, saying that memory is necessary to familiarity as a part of it, but is saying that memory is necessary to familiarity as a precondition of it: there is in the notion of familiarity an element, namely pastness, which we could not obtain unless remembering were, at least sometimes, something more than having images tinged with familiarity.

That this objection too is invalid can be shown in two ways. The first way is to point out that a direct acquaintance with a previous event no more explains our having the notion of pastness than it is explained by familiarity itself; it would leave it as much a mystery as before. The peculiar thing about memory is not that it produces the past for me, but that it produces it *as* the past. Marconi was reported to have had the ambition of constructing a radio set that would pick up sound waves long after they had been emitted, and perhaps eventually to pick up Christ delivering the Sermon on the Mount. Such a radio would be producing the past for the listener, but would not be producing it *as* the past; provided that the set was sufficiently sensitive and selective there would be nothing about what the listener heard which would lead him to suppose that he was not hearing words a second or so after they were being spoken in a studio somewhere. Similarly, if remembering were simply a direct cognitive relation with a previous experience, it would not at all account for our having the notion of pastness. Memory cannot be argued to be a precondition of familiarity on the ground that something would be left unexplained if it were not, unless that something would be explained if it were; but, as we have just seen, it would be no better explained at all.

## 6. The notion of past is empirical

Secondly, while admitting that pastness is an essential element in the notion of familiarity, we can, I think, explain it without having recourse to memory. The fact is that a man can acquire the notion of pastness in precisely the same way as he acquires the notion of red, viz. empirically, by seeing an instance of it. We acquire the notion of red by having red things pointed out to us and by having them distinguished from green or blue things, from jagged things, noisy things, etc. So, if we come across instances of pastness, which can be sufficiently distinguished from instances of other concepts, we can acquire the notion of pastness. Surely we are constantly coming across cases of pastness, namely, whenever we are aware of a duration of time. To say that something is past is to say that it occurred before something else; and we are aware of one thing happening before another whenever, for instance, we see any movement, such as a cat walking across the floor. Whatever the ophthalmologists may say, we do see continuous movement in such a case, i.e. we are within a given present aware of a limited duration within which the cat walks from right to left. The present is not for our awareness an instantaneous click of a camera shutter with no perceptible duration. It has a perceptible duration, within which we are aware that one stage precedes another, in other words, within which we are aware of an instance of pastness.

No doubt, too much has been claimed on behalf of this perceptible duration, so as to make its technical title of 'the Specious Present' unfortunately apt, but it is hard to see what grounds there are for denying its occurrence. Questions such as how long it lasts, what variations in length it can have between one person and another, or between different states of alertness in one person interest psychologists rather than philosophers. But that it does vary in length, and that there is a borderland of uncertainty which one cannot clearly allot either to present perception as against memory, or *vice versa*, suggest that the distinction between experience of the present and memory of the past may be a gradual merging, and that the point at which one makes the cut is a matter of convenience or convention. Listening to a clock striking I may still hear the first stroke when I hear the second; if a man says something to me I may, because I am not attending, not hear what he says and ask him to say it again— and yet I may, before he repeats himself, still manage to catch what he said. As I read a book, the portion of a sentence that I can take in at once will depend on among other things the degree of my fatigue, of my interest in the book, and of the book's difficulty for me—i.e. the extent to which I depend on memory will vary with varying conditions.

Of course, to say that the concept of pastness is acquired in the same way as the concept of redness, namely empirically, does not involve saying that there are no important differences between the two or between the conditions of their acquisition. Pastness is an all-pervading concept, while redness is a casual concept; that is to say, a man might go through life without ever acquiring the concept of red at all, e.g. if he were blind or if he were not blind but never saw anything red nor heard 'red' mentioned. His experience would be deficient in one respect, but would hardly be affected at all in others. Pastness, on the other hand, seems necessary to our having at all the sort of experience that we do have; it is, as it were, part of the pattern of experience as opposed to any of the elements or contents arranged in that pattern. All the contents of a man's experience might have been different from what they are, and yet the experience would still have been a human experience. But the arrangement of experience into a temporal pattern of before and after could not be different and still leave it as an experience, in any sense in which we use that word. Nevertheless, that our experience has to be arranged in the pattern of before and after does not preclude our acquiring our concept of pastness empirically. Therefore, once more, the admitted fact that pastness is an element in the notion of familiarity can be accounted for, without requiring memory of some other kind as a precondition of familiarity.[1]

## 7. *Familiarity is no guarantee*

The familiarity theory thus does avoid the objections which we found in the case of Hume were fatal to any such simple theory as that which makes remembering consist of having images which resemble their originals. For the familiarity theory does account for our having the notion of pastness, for our supposing that there is a past at all, and for our referring some images and not others to the

1. C. D. Broad in his *Mind and its Place in Nature*, pp. 266–7, seems to argue that (i) to have the notion of pastness because pastness is categorial or part of the pattern of experience, and (ii) to have it as an empirically acquired concept obtained from the specious present are exclusive alternatives, between which a philosopher must decide; he himself is inclined to favour (i). But he offers no reason why we should suppose that they are alternatives at all, let alone exclusive alternatives.

past in the peculiar way in which memory does. It does not, however, offer any guarantee that any memory is ever right. The fact that some of my images feel familiar, while others do not, may lead me to claim that, in the case of the first, I am remembering something from my past, but in itself it provides no sort of guarantee that my memories are correct. It offers no reason why we should trust those images which feel familiar rather than those which do not. Yet we all do clearly trust the former rather than the latter. This comes out particularly clearly when one is trying to remember something, but having very great difficulty doing it; and it applies equally well to any images, regardless of the sense to which they belong.

Suppose, for instance, that I for some reason or other want to remember the name of a man whom I used to know but have not seen for years; I may be able to visualise him very clearly, to recollect a number of contexts in which I had dealings with him, to remember what his voice sounded like, what a clammy handshake he had, how his breath smelt slightly of whisky, and so on—and yet I cannot recall his name. I try out name after name, but none of them seems to fit, none feels right; I may feel certain that it is a short name beginning with a G, or that it is a Cornish sounding name of some kind—but none of the clues leads anywhere; it is an infuriating experience, in which the harder one tries the more hopeless the task becomes. Then suddenly, when one is not trying at all, a name comes into the mind and falls into place almost with a click—it was Tread-gold (not Cornish at all, but the first three letters made it look a bit like it; and it was the second syllable, not the first, that began with a G); it fits at once, and one is quite sure that it is the right name. Now the difference between this name and all the others suggested and rejected is simply that this one feels right, while all the others did not. We are convinced of this name, as we were unconvinced of the others. But, if we are sceptically inclined, we may ask what sort of guarantee a feeling of familiarity provides. It certainly is not a gilt-edge guarantee, because we have no difficulty in thinking of cases where the images did have the familiar feeling about them, and yet what we claim to remember never happened; I might, for instance, be convinced by the familiarity test that my man's name was Treadgold, but still be wrong, as I would be if Treadgold was the name, not of that man, but of another closely associated with him, so that I constantly saw the two together and subsequently confused their names. Does familiarity then provide, if not a gilt-edge guarantee, at least a reasonable working criterion that the memory is correct? Can we infer from the fact that a certain set of images have a feeling of being familiar that it is highly probable that we are remembering correctly? Strictly, we cannot. For we should need to have some cases in which, when we have memory-images, two conditions are fulfilled: (a) we *knew* that our remembering was correct; (b) the images felt familiar.

If we could find some cases in which both conditions were fulfilled, then that would provide some probability that we were remembering correctly in other cases where only the second condition was fulfilled. That is to say, the familiarity of images would provide some evidence that we were remembering correctly, as long as at least in some cases we not only had the feeling of familiarity, but also and independently knew that we were remembering correctly. Unfortunately, if the familiarity theory is true, condition (a) is never fulfilled; for, if remembering consists of having images marked by familiarity, how could we know by some other remembering that the remembering was correct? and how else could we know but by remembering? The difficulty is reminiscent of one that we found Hume raising against the first form of the simple image theory.[1]

It might be argued that although familiarity cannot be proba-bilified in that way, yet there are at least two other ways in which it can be done. According to the first, which might be called the Prediction Method, familiarity is probabilified by its enabling us to make accurate predictions. If I do treat my memories as correct and base my predictions on them, I shall make fewer mistakes both theoretical and practical than if I do not treat them as accurate. For instance, I might reasonably claim to remember that nowadays motor-cars travel at such a speed that pedestrians who have stepped in front of them have lived to regret it or have not lived at all. If I base my conduct on the supposition that that memory is correct, I shall probably live longer than if I do not. The success of familiarity

1. p. 41 above.

memory, then, is some evidence, and strong evidence, that the memory is correct.

Now nobody, I think, would be so absurd as to deny the facts—that a life guided by past memories is less likely to be cut short by a motor-car than one not so guided—and I would not be thought to be denying them. But it is not clear that they really do substantiate the familiarity theory. What we are trying to do is to provide some evidence, compatible with memory consisting of having images plus a feeling of familiarity, that such memories are usually or often (or even only sometimes) correct. And the evidence provided is that if such memories are used in directing one's future one's future is less dangerous. But the use of the evidence itself is a case of memory. All collection of evidence, all theories, depend on memory, as Descartes found to his distress when he was trying to elaborate an error-proof method of attaining knowledge in any sphere.[1] In this case, if I work out my reason for (that is, the reason that would justify me in) trusting my familiarity memory in a particular case to be a relevant and helpful guide to the future, I find it is that I remember that such memories have been helpful guides in the past. Once more the reliability of memory is depending on memory. What we were trying to do was to probabilify that familiarity memory is correct; but of course we do not probabilify it by producing simply a further case of familiarity memory. That merely sets us off on an unending regress; the correctness of memory cannot be probabilified that way, if having images plus the feeling of familiarity is all that remembering consists of.

The other method that might be (and has been) suggested of probabilifying familiarity memory is what might be called the Diary Method. I find that while my images are divisible into those which feel familiar and those which do not, the first set correspond to entries in my diary, while the latter do not; or, more accurately, I find that some of the first set correspond (for not everything which I may remember is likely to be recorded in my diary), while none of the second set corresponds. My diary enables me to check my past and reveals that on the whole familiarity images are accurate, while there is no evidence at all to suggest that the other images are. Thus the

1. *Meditations* v, *Regulae* vii.

entries in my diary probabilify the correctness of my memory, and the longer the correspondence between my memories and my diary continues, and the more detailed it is, the greater is the probability of the correctness of memory. Here, again, the facts are not in dispute: we do use diaries and other documents to check our memories, and within varying but specifiable limits it is a perfectly proper thing to do. But, once again, it does not help the familiarity theory. For the entries in my diary are worthless as evidence to check my memories unless I have reason for supposing that my diary is in general a truthful record of what happened. And how else ultimately can I suppose that, except by remembering—by remembering, for instance, that at that period I kept a diary and took pains to make the entries accurate? From this point on, the objections to the Diary Method are the same as those to the Prediction Method, and need not be repeated.

We have now reached the point at which we can see that the familiarity theory of memory, although it escapes many of the objections to which the simpler dualist theory with which we started was prone, yet fails to escape the fundamental difficulties of dualism —summarily, that if it alone is the true account of memory, not only do we not have the intimate knowledge of our past experience (or parts of it) that we all in fact suppose we do have, but we have not even the right to rely on our memories in the way in which we all do and cannot help doing. This is an unwelcome conclusion which none of us, except when philosophising, would be willing or able to rest in; and before we resign ourselves to accepting it, we should consider whether there is any other possible theory of memory. It would be impossible not to feel some sympathy with the man who, having been buried in the debris of an air raid, and having been told by his rescuer (who was interested in the Theory of Memory) that he did not really *know* that he had been buried, replied: 'If *that's* not knowing, I would like to know what is.'

# 3

## MEMORY (continued)

### 1. Naïve Realism

Let us now look at the other of the two alternative theories of memory which we earlier attributed to the plain man, the theory called Naïve Realism, according to which an act of memory has for its cognitive object the actual event remembered. We suggested there that although it was an ordinary man's view, it was probably less attractive to him than the other view which we have been discussing, because, for the most part, we do not tend to believe that when we remember the past is literally recalled and presented before us. That was an overstatement, which may have helped to make the issue clearer, but which needs some correction now. The fact is that as ordinary men, while we do believe that we remember via images, we do not distinguish between an image and the event remembered; perhaps we are quite right in not making the distinction (I shall suggest shortly that we are), but even if we are wrong that would not alter the fact (if it be one) that we do not make it. That is to say, from the fact that we do ordinarily suppose that remembering is done via images it does not follow that we are not Naïve Realists.

If what we ordinarily suppose is in any way evidence relevant to the solution of a philosophical problem, then we must not blink the fact that quite often we ordinarily suppose two (or more) quite different and incompatible things on the same subject. If a philosopher can show that we ordinarily suppose A about a certain subject, he is not entitled to infer that in that case we do not ordinarily suppose

B, which is incompatible with A; it is unfortunately an inference which philosophers are only too ready to draw, when they look to our ordinary beliefs. Professor Broad hints at this point in his discussion of memory already referred to, but he believes nevertheless that we are not ordinarily Naïve Realists in our remembering, as we certainly are in our perceiving. 'Naïve Realism,' he says, 'is not merely a *theory about* perception; it is the explicit formulation of the belief which forms *an essential part* of the perceptual situation as such. But Naïve Realism is merely a *theory about* memory.'[1] Here I find myself unable to agree with him: the difference between perception and memory as regards Naïve Realism is surely one of emphasis only. It is not that a perceptual judgment is naïvely realistic, while a memory judgment in itself is not; it is rather that, normally at any rate, the contents of the present impinge on us much more forcibly than the contents of the past, and that the prime function of memory is to play second fiddle to perception. But where memories are especially forcible, as some are for most of us—e.g. the memory of a particularly very enjoyable, or a terrifying, or a highly embarrassing experience—they are as naïvely realistic (in Professor Broad's sense) as any perceptual experience.

Mercifully, memories do not usually crowd in on us the way perceptions do, and they do not usually push themselves on our attention as demandingly; for that we may be thankful, at the same time realising that their moderation is only a matter of degree. We have no ground for saying that while Naïve Realism is a part of a perceptual judgment it is not part of a memory judgment, but only a theory about it. However, while not admitting that we are not realists in our memory judgments, we should not, even if we did admit it, abandon realism on that account. The brief discussion in Chapter 1 suggested that we were wrong in being Naïve Realists over perception; it might equally well turn out that we would not be wrong to be Naïve Realists over memory.

## 2. The objection from time

The first and most obvious objection to the view that the immediate object of remembering is the event remembered is the objection

1. *Mind and its Place in Nature*, p. 243.

alluded to earlier, that of time. How, it is asked, can I possibly have before my mind literally an event, or part of it, which occurred, say, ten years ago? When the event happened, it ceased to exist; and in any case, how could an event in my mind which is occurring now (the act of remembering) bridge the time interval so as to have for its object another event which is not occurring now, but finished occurring ten years ago? Now this objection, psychologically powerful though it may be, seems to me quite worthless. For what is the evidence for it? It is not empirical, i.e. it does not consist of citing cases where the immediate object of remembering is clearly not the object remembered. For, if we could cite such cases, then the question of the relation of thing remembered to act of remembering would never have arisen; we should not even be wondering whether the relationship could be such that the one was the immediate object of the other. Indeed, what possible empirical evidence could one imagine oneself discovering that would answer or help to answer this particular epistemological question? We need to distinguish two cases, which might be confused:

(i) The case in which there may or may not be direct acquaintance with the past, but which is *not* a case of memory.

(ii) The case in which there may or may not be direct acquaintance with the past, and which *is* a case of memory.

An example of (i) would be provided by the adventure of the two Oxford ladies who, when walking round the gardens of the Palace of Versailles in 1901, were struck both by a number of features in the gardens and by the appearance of other persons walking about. The latter were all dressed in the clothes appropriate to the reign of Louis XVI; and investigation of records later revealed that certain artificial features of the gardens which the ladies had clearly observed, such as a grotto and a small ravine with a bridge across it, were features which did exist at the time of Marie Antoinette, but were some fifty years later cleared away. In other words, what the visitors had seen in 1901 was the garden, not as it was in 1901, but as it was a hundred years earlier in 1789, peopled exactly as it was at that time. Certainly metaphorically and perhaps literally, the two visitors had been transported back a hundred years into the past. Now the authenticity of this adventure does not concern us, although in fact the evidence has been most carefully and dispassionately collected,[1] but what does interest us is that it purports to be an instance of some kind of acquaintance with the past which is not also an instance of memory. There is no suggestion that the two ladies, in having that experience, were remembering anything from *their* past. What they saw and watched did not seem familiar in that sense at all, and they were not tempted to suppose that they were remembering. What they were tempted to suppose was that the gardens which they saw, complete with guards, cloaked strangers and a lady sketching, were the gardens at the time of seeing them; and that they were not the gardens as they were at the time of seeing them the visitors were able to establish empirically, after the experience was over, by noticing the gardens as they actually were, and observing that the topography was different. Summing up this instance we may say that the characteristic feature of such a case is that, at the time of its occurring, the content of the experience seems to belong to the present (or, what comes to the same thing, that the experient is unconsciously transported to the past), but that afterwards it can be established on empirical grounds not to belong to the present. The grotto, ravine, bridge, and wood were, according to the records, cleared away many years ago, and no trace of them is now to be found in the location where the two ladies saw them, and where contemporary maps show that they originally stood.

Case (ii), on the other hand, of which any memory will provide an instance, while like case (i) in being retrocognitive, is unlike it in an important respect, that at the time of having the retrocognition one thinks of it *as* being retrocognitive. What a man remembers he is not tempted to locate in the present and only afterwards on empirical grounds to date somewhere in the past; part of the actual experience of remembering *is* to date the event remembered somewhere in the past. Now, what empirical evidence, acquired from the nature of one's experience of the present, could show that what seemed to be an experience of the past in the way that memory seems was not in fact an experience of the past at all, except in an indirect and elliptical sense?

1. *An Adventure* by Elizabeth Morison and F. Lamont; *The Trianon Case* by Landale Johnston.

It is surely clear that the argument that remembering cannot have for its direct object the event remembered is an *a priori* argument, based not on the collection of evidence nor on the citing of cases, but on a theory, about the nature of time. It is supposed that when something happens, it has then happened, and is thereafter as unavailable for subsequent observation as it was for previous observation before it happened, just as if I do not see the lightning flash when it occurs I cannot hope to see it afterwards (for it is no longer there to see). It is further supposed that, even if we waived the first difficulty, we would still have to allow that no part of a present experience can fall outside the present; I can only experience what is contemporary with the experience itself, and consequently an act of remembering cannot have as its direct object an event not contemporary with but prior to itself. Now, neither of these suppositions seems one which we must accept; they are not self-evident principles, nor are they deducible from self-evident principles; and, as we saw earlier,[1] even in the case of perception itself it seems that we have to allow that what is perceived is not contemporary with the act of perceiving it. In fact, the argument from time against the suggestion that memory has for its direct object the event remembered is revealed on examination to rest on nothing more solid than confusion and unreflective prejudice.[2]

### 3. *The objection from discrepancy between image and event remembered*

We come now to a rather more serious difficulty. If Naïve Realism were true, would it be possible for a memory-image to differ from the event remembered? The two, certainly on occasions and perhaps often, clearly do seem to differ, either when the image is fairly but not completely like the thing remembered, or when it is not at all like it. As an instance of the first, I may remember an incident in a cricket match in which I played, and I may have a clear pictorial image— the shape of the ground, the position and appearance of the pavilion, the line of houses beyond, the distribution of the fielding side, and so

1. See p. 20 above.
2. For a fuller discussion of this argument, see Broad, *Mind and its Place in Nature*, pp. 251–6.

on. But, if the fielders were not in fact distributed as they are according to my image, am I in remembering directly cognising the past
incident which I remember? Again, not only may my image not
resemble the event in some respect or other, but I may, even while
remembering, feel sure that it does not. Let us suppose that the
incident was of the batsman pulling the ball hard to square leg and
hitting the umpire on the ankle; in my image the umpire's visible
clothes are a pair of dark brown shoes, grey flannel trousers, a long
white umpire's coat, a nondescript coloured shirt and a bow tie.
Now, even while having that image, I am sure that the bow tie, the
shirt, and the coat are right. I am sure that the trousers are wrong,
and about the shoes I have no very clear idea at all. There, then, is a
case where at the same time as remembering I may rightly believe
(for I *am* right in this case) not only that my image is wrong in a
certain respect, but also in which respect it is wrong.

The other case which is relevant is the case where the image does
not appear at all to resemble the event remembered. For myself, this
is a case which does not occur, because it would happen chiefly with
non-pictorial images, while all my remembering is done with pictorial
images. However, I am ready to believe that not everyone (quite
apart from the blind, who are in this instance irrelevant) remembers
wholly with pictorial images: some may depend mainly on descriptive
word images, i.e. either of the visual appearance or of the sound of
the words. I do not feel qualified to discuss such cases, simply
because they do not happen to me; my remembering often enough
does involve word images of either sort, but only, I think, in those
cases where words were an element in the event remembered—as
when I remember Mr Chamberlain's tired voice announcing over
the radio the declaration of war on 3 September 1939, or when I
remember reading the 1945 general election results in a newspaper.
They are not apparent exceptions to the realist account, because they
are in the relevant sense pictorial. What is wanted is an instance of
an episode, in which or about which no words were spoken, written,
or read, but which is now remembered not via resembling, but via
verbal imagery. As I have said, remembering of that sort does not
seem to happen to me, but I am not prepared to infer from that that
it can happen to nobody.

Do these cases—and to them should be added the case of error, of misremembering—dispose of the realist theory of memory? If in remembering one is directly retrocognising the event remembered, how could the imagery be slightly wrong, or how could it be quite dissimilar (in kind) from the event remembered, or how could I be mistaken in my memories? *Prima facie* they appear to destroy the theory, but I am not quite sure that they do. It is not an easy question to answer, because it depends on what the realist theory exactly is a theory about; and that itself it not completely clear. On the one hand, if the theory says that remembering *consists* simply of some direct retrocognitive acquaintance with the past (different in an unspecified way from the retrocognition experienced by the ladies at Versailles), then the examples above do destroy it. On the other hand, if the theory says that remembering *involves* such direct acquaintance with the past, but does not consist only of that, then it may hope to breathe again. These two alternatives need to be clearly distinguished. Here, indeed is a prime example of that philosophical danger referred to earlier, viz., the ease with which one can get into a muddle through not being clear what exactly the question is that one is trying to answer.

Let us consider these two questions:

(a) In remembering am I directly aware of a past event?

(b) In remembering do I always know?

The temptation to suppose that an affirmative answer to (a) requires an affirmative answer to (b) is perhaps natural; and correspondingly natural is the conclusion that because the answer to (b) is certainly negative (for we often do make mistakes in remembering), the answer to (a) must be negative, too. But in fact, as I hope to explain, we could answer (a) affirmatively without thereby determining the answer to (b); consequently a negative answer to (b), which we certainly must give, does not automatically decide the answer to (a).

## 4. Does remembering involve direct acquaintance with the past?

Question (a) is a question about what may be called the *materials* of memory judgments. We saw that if we treat these materials as being present images numerically different from, but more or less accurate reproductions of, the past events remembered via them, no

reason could be given why we should suppose them to be reproductions, or why we should ever prefer one to another; we should
be caught, with no hope of escape, in the trap of images. Are we
then in the opposite but corresponding trap, if we say that the
materials of memory are the events remembered? Have we, by saying
that, extruded images and once more proved ourselves wrong? For
it would not be denied that images do occur in memory, although
some might deny that they are necessary to it. My own suggestion
is that they are necessary, but that they are not to be regarded as
entities at all. It is surely a fact that we are not normally in danger
of confusing remembering with perceiving, although we may sometimes mistake it for imagining or *vice versa*; and what chiefly distinguishes remembering from perceiving is the presence in the one and
the absence from the other of images. No doubt in extreme cases,
e.g. exceptional fatigue or drunkenness or delirium, perceptual
situations may occur which the percipient will not know whether to
describe in terms of images or not. But language seldom does provide
satisfactorily for the extreme circumstances; no doubt, if they
became sufficiently frequent to constitute a new normality, we should
have to adjust our language to them, and we should have a puzzling
time doing it. However, until that occurs, the normal cases are
those in which we do not feel tempted to confuse perceiving with
remembering, or to talk of having images in the first and not to talk
of having them in the second.

I can see no reason for supposing that there are events, persons,
and things on the one hand, and on the other hand more or less
pallid mental reflections of them called images. The supposition that
all images are, as it were, portraits in a mirror, is due more to
obedience to a word than to attention to what is referred to by that
word. Some images are indeed reflections, more or less accurate, of
their originals, e.g. what is seen when one looks into a pool or a
mirror. But would we suppose, if we considered memory-images
dispassionately and by themselves, that they were images in at all
the same sense? Images in water and glass are seen in exactly the
same way as their originals are seen, except that they are seen in
water and glass instead of three-dimensionally. But the manner of
experiencing them is not different: whatever we mean by 'see' in

'seeing a tree', we mean just the same thing by it in 'seeing the reflection of a tree in water'. The cognitive relation is the same, while the objects in each case are different in kind and numerically different; for one thing, their spatial locations are different. Now, none of this appears to be true of a memory-image and its original; if we think it is, that is because we are already giving credence to a theory, however little explicit, about the nature of memory; but it is no theory that leads us to distinguish between the image of a tree in the water and the tree itself standing on the bank. Having a memory-image is not at all like, let alone the same as, the original experience of seeing (or otherwise perceiving) the event now remembered. What seems peculiar to memory is not the materials of it, but the cognitive relation involved; and the image is not a *thing* at all distinct numerically from the thing remembered (I am speaking here only of correct memory).

As with so many other psychological names (e.g. 'the will', 'a desire', 'conscience', etc.), we are very easily misled by 'image' being a noun word into supposing that it is the name of, the label for, a thing or entity of some special kind, just as 'table', 'baboon', and 'poached egg' are names of entities each of some special kind. But we must not be misled by words. What the word 'image' stands for here is a certain mode of awareness, the way an object appears when it enters into a memory situation (or imagination situation). Because in remembering we are trying to recall the original event as it was at the time of its occurring, we are led to distinguish between it as it looked then and it as it looks now; while such a distinction is natural and valid enough, we have no ground whatever for going on to make the further distinction of treating the original as one *thing* and the present memory-image as another *thing*. If we see that there is no case for this latter distinction, we find that many of the traditional puzzles over memory disappear, namely all the puzzles of dualism generated by the supposed imitative relation holding between a memory-image and its original; if we start by inventing *things* of a peculiar sort, which do not in fact exist, and by calling them images, we are bound to store up insoluble puzzles for ourselves; but if we realise that images are not things at all, different from their originals, the puzzles which depended on their being things disappear.

One more point needs making, before the suggestion which I am putting forward about images can claim any plausibility; and it is a point which brings us on to question (b) on p. 60 above. Although on this theory of memory I am always when remembering directly in contact with originals, I may not be in contact with *the* original which I am claiming to remember. If in remembering my umpire being hit on the ankle I remember that he was wearing grey flannel trousers, when in fact he was not, I am muddling two different originals, my umpire and some man or other who on that or some other occasion associated with it in my mind was wearing grey flannel trousers. In short, although the materials of remembering are always originals, they do not need to be the originals which I think they are; and that is the reason why, if we answer question (a) on p. 60 affirmatively, as I have suggested that we should, it does not commit us also to giving an affirmative answer to question (b), but leaves that open, to be answered on its own merits.

## 5. *Is remembering always knowing?*

Question (b) is a question not about the *materials* but about the *validity* of memory judgments. And in the most ordinary sense of the word 'remember' the answer must be No. It is perfectly true that we do often use 'remember' in such a way that we would not say that 'I remember X happening' was correct, if X never happened. *Before* being shown that X never happened, I might say, 'I remember X happening,' and *afterwards* I should say, 'I could have sworn that I remembered X happening, but I admit now that I must have been wrong.' In other words, after being shown that a particular memory judgment is false, we are inclined to say that in that case it could not have been memory at all, but something else which we mistook for memory. In this sense we are using 'memory' in such a way that memory cannot be wrong, that we will withhold the name 'memory' if it is wrong. But in this sense question (b) becomes a wholly trivial and uninteresting question, asking, 'Provided that "I remember" is used only on those occasions when I remember correctly, is remembering always a case of knowing?' If by definition remembering cannot be wrong, then, provided that I know that it cannot be wrong, remembering must be a case of knowing—but only because

I have by definition refused to call it remembering unless the memory is correct. But that, of course, proves nothing, except perhaps that philosophical problems cannot be settled in that way by definitions.

What that illustration does bring out is nevertheless something important, namely that the truth of a man's statement, 'I remember . . .' does not necessarily depend on his memory being correct, let alone on his knowing that it is correct, but on something else; we use 'I remember . . .' as corresponding not only to 'I know . . .' but also to 'I believe . . .'. While the truth of a man's statement, 'I know . . .' does depend on the rest of his statement being correct (for we do not allow that a man could know something which was false), the same does not apply to 'I believe . . .'. 'I know it is raining' must be false if it is not raining, but 'I believe it is raining' need not be false if it is not raining; for to the truth of 'I believe it is raining' the question whether it is actually raining or not is irrelevant—what does matter is whether the man *thinks* it is. Similarly, we do not deny the title 'memory judgment' to a judgment merely because the judgment is false; we do, after all, talk of memory playing queer tricks, which we would not if we thought that all memory judgments must be true.

The answer, then, to (*b*) is twofold. (i) If by 'remembering' we insist on meaning 'remembering correctly' (as we *sometimes* do), the answer is Yes. But it is then an uninteresting question, and the interesting question instead is, 'How can we tell a memory from what looks like but is not a memory—i.e. a false memory judgment?'

(ii) If by 'remembering' we mean 'making a memory judgment', then the answer is No. Maybe our language would be tidier if we always meant one thing and not the other (it would not matter which) by 'remember', but the fact must be faced that we do mean both, and that sometimes we would be hard put to it to say which of the two, as opposed to the other, we do mean. (On either version, incidentally, a man may be wrong when he *says* 'I remember X', even when he honestly believes that he does remember it. The difference comes in when he *truthfully* says 'I remember X': on version (i) he cannot, on version (ii) he still can, be wrong.)

## 6. Is remembering ever knowing?

I prefer to use 'memory' in sense (ii), in the wider sense which covers all memory judgments, true or false. In that sense, as we have seen, remembering is not always knowing, for we frequently misremember. In this sense, is remembering *ever* knowing? The extreme sceptic is inclined to deny that it is, for instance on the ground that we have no stronger reason for supposing the past to be as we remember it to have been than we have for supposing the future will be what we think it will be. The sceptic is, I think, inclined to confuse himself, and to suppose that one cannot know anything unless what is known is *necessarily* true, i.e. could not without self-contradiction be asserted to be otherwise. Now, if he insists on restricting knowledge in that way, then of course one cannot know that the future will be of a certain sort: although it is true that the sun will rise in the east tomorrow, it is not necessarily true; there is no logical contradiction involved in the suggestion that it will rise in the west for a change, but only a disturbing surprise in store for us (that is, if we could survive the earth's change of direction during the night).

Therefore, in the sceptic's sense of 'know', even although it is in fact true that the sun will rise in the east tomorrow (that it is true you will discover tomorrow), it is not a logically necessary truth, and therefore cannot be known. It is logically possible that a number of queer and uncomfortable things may happen tonight to prevent the sun rising in the east. Similarly with memory: although our memories of the past interlock and confirm each other in the thorough and systematic way that they do, we may be, i.e. it is logically possible that we are, all making the same mistake. In that sense of 'may', all our memories may be illusory, and we could only describe it as fortunate both that our sets of illusions fit in with each other and that they enable us to go on living; we might, after all, have had a completely different set of illusory memories, leading us to treat motor-cars, snorting bulls, and other lethal instruments with far less respect than we do.

If this is what the sceptic wishes to say—that we can know nothing except what is logically necessary—and if what he wishes to say is true, then it does follow that remembering is not a way of our knowing; for although many of my memory judgments may be in

C

fact true, none of them is logically necessary. And if memory falls to the sceptical axe, so also does a great deal else of what ordinarily passes for knowledge: as I walk across the downs and feel drops of water falling on my head I do not know it is raining; hearing the radio announcement of Princess Elizabeth's wedding and reading of it in the newspapers I do not know that she is married; seeing a man jump over Westminster Bridge I do not know that he will reach the water. None of these things, according to the sceptic, do I know, for none is logically necessary: feeling water on my face is logically compatible with its coming out of a concealed garden hose or an invisible watering can; it is logically possible that the B B C and the Press have conspired in a gigantic hoax (or themselves been the victims of one) to embarrass the monarchy; it is logically possible that the law of gravity will cease to operate, that the falling man will vanish into thin air or turn into a bird. How little knowledge the sceptic would leave us with the reader may work out for himself; memory at least will not find itself in a specially unprivileged position.

All this follows from accepting the sceptic's initial premise, that nothing can be known unless it is a logically necessary truth. But is there any reason why we should be required to accept this premise, to confine knowledge within such a cramped strait-jacket? True, there is such a thing as knowledge of a necessary truth; but what reason has the sceptic for saying that that is the only kind of knowledge that there is? We may, if we like, legislate by decree that the word 'know' shall only be used where what is apprehended is a necessary truth, but then we shall have to go to the trouble of finding another word to cover the other ways in which we now use the word 'know'. We have not thereby shown that memory is not a way of knowing; all we shall have done will be to lay down that as memory does not apprehend necessary truths (for this is admitted), by our new convention of language, which confines 'know' to the apprehension of necessary truths, 'know' and 'knowledge' are linguistically inappropriate words for use in descriptions of remembering. Whether remembering is ever a way of knowing is to be decided, not by a linguistic *fiat*, but by (*a*) giving an analysis of knowledge (which will, of course, involve statements about language), and (*b*) deciding whether memory ever satisfies the conditions of that analysis.

What we want is to be able to distinguish knowing from not knowing, e.g. from believing, and then to see how the distinction affects memory judgments. The problem then of memory judgments is only a special case of the problem of the validity of belief in general, and of the distinction between knowledge and belief. What is required is that distinction and a criterion for making it.[1] It will not be a criterion which I can always successfully apply to my memories so as to get the right answer. For if it were such a criterion, it would have the consequence that I could always tell by inspecting a memory situation whether it was a case of knowing or not; and that as I know (again by memory) I cannot always do. The only way in which I can insure with certainty against never *wrongly* claiming to know by memory is by never claiming to know by memory at all; and that is a heavier premium than I am prepared to pay, or than anyone else is, I think, prepared to pay.

1. This is discussed in chapter 8. It should not be necessary to point out that, although some remembering is knowing, not all knowing about the past is remembering. I know many things about the past, even about *my* past, which I do not remember. The question about memory being knowledge is not whether what I claim to remember did happen to me or not, but whether my claim to remember it is correct or not.

# 4

## UNIVERSALS

### 1. General words

Language is so much the most commonly used of all our tools for the continuance and improvement of our lives, for the promotion of our interests, and often enough for the obstruction of others' interests, that we normally take it for granted and show no curiosity about its features or its efficiency. We think, quite rightly, if we even ask ourselves the question what its function is, that it is to provide a means of communicating our thoughts to each other; we would not be right if we said that that was its only function, for clearly it is not, but we would be right in saying that that is one of its prime functions. And the efficiency with which it discharges that function depends very largely on its generality. We want to be able to talk about objects that are not present at the time of speaking, and we want to talk about groups or collections of objects. Extension of thought beyond the immediately here and now is only made possible by the presence in a language of general words. Indeed, if we put on one side proper names (e.g. 'John Brown', and 'Washington, D C') and indicator words such as 'this' and 'that', all the remaining words in the English language are general.

Even proper names, in the sense illustrated, have their aspect of generality, for we say, for instance, that there are far more John Browns in the world than there are Montague Pinchingtons, and again that there is more than one place called Washington; for that reason, if we want to make it clear that we are referring to the capital of the U S A we add the initials D C; and even then we allow that there *might* be more than one place called Washington, D C. But most words do not even appear to be the names of one particular person or one particular place; their whole point and usefulness is that they can be applied to any one of a whole range of objects or activities, e.g. 'table', 'horse', 'delphinium', 'write', 'dislike', 'underneath', 'obscurely', and so on, throughout the dictionary.

If a stranger with whom I fall into conversation in an hotel complains of the low standard of comfort which the hotel provides and says by way of instance, 'One of the legs on the armchair in my bedroom is missing', I understand perfectly well what he means by the statement, even though I have not seen his chair nor know which is his bedroom. I understand what he means, because all the words in his statement (except in a special sense 'my') are general words: 'armchair' is the name not of the particular armchair he is referring to, but of any armchair at all; 'missing' is the name not of a particular feature of the particular situation of which he is complaining, but of a feature which is common and peculiar to all situations from which something is missing; and so also of the other words in the sentence. Consequently, as long as I know what an armchair is, what a leg is, what it is for something to be missing, etc., I shall understand his statement, and I shall be able to make a suitable reply.

Thanks to the generality of words, we do not need to have had personal experience of an object or a state of affairs before we may understand and make statements about it. Still more obviously is this the case where the statement is a general statement, e.g. a causal statement, such as 'Electricity costs are governed by coal costs.' In making that statement I am not making a historical assertion about the way in which my electricity bills have risen as miners' wages have risen. I am not making an assertion about any *particular* situation at all, although I may either have many such assertions in mind at the time or be able to produce them as evidence for my statement if challenged. My statement itself is a generalisation, asserting that wherever coal costs fluctuate electricity costs fluctuate correspondingly; I am supposing it to refer not merely to all past cases of fluctuations in coal costs, but to any future cases as well. It is in fact what has sometimes been called an 'open' statement, because it refers not to any one particular situation or to a number of particular situations, but to all (or any) situations *of a certain sort*. To understand my statement and to refute it (e.g. by calling my attention to hydro-electric systems) you do not need ever to have paid an electricity bill in your life. Thanks again to the generality of words, as long as you know what electricity and coal are (in the sense in which most people reading this book are likely to know what they are), and how the cost of one thing can depend on the cost of something else, you will understand my statement, 'Electricity costs are governed by coal costs.'

## 2. Are general words names of universals?

From a very early period in the history of thought philosophers have found problems in the generality of words. It is easy enough to see what a proper name is the name of, viz. the particular person or place whose name it is. But what is a general word, such as 'table' or 'missing', the name of? True, philosophers have not always, although they have often, approached the problem from the angle of language. Disregarding the words of any given language, experience provides us with many instances of exact or approximate repetitions of earlier experiences: in the course of a man's life he sees many tables, and recognises them all as tables. Each of them is particular, in that he sees it at some specific time and place, and in that sense every table is different from every other; they may be qualitatively different, too, varying in shape or size or colour or number of legs, etc.; but despite the numerical differences which there must be and the qualitative differences which there may be, there is a certain form or pattern common to them all, that they are all tables.

Hence, we get the traditional metaphysical picture of the world, as made up of individual substances, each characterised by its attributes, the essential difference between the two being that a substance is a particular belonging to only one place at any one time, while an attribute may belong to a variety of places at a time, according as whether there are substances characterised by it in each of those places at that time. Whereas the particular table which is in my dining-room now is not now, and cannot now, also be somewhere else, the attribute of being a table simultaneously belongs to the object in my dining-room, to a couple of others in my kitchen, another in my bedroom, and, in fact, to all the objects at present existing anywhere which are tables. The distinction between a substance and its attributes has traditionally been known as the distinction between particulars and universals. For approximately the last two thousand five hundred years philosophers have been asking themselves what universals are. What philosophers have been asking for is not examples of universals, but a definition of a universal, an answer to the question what sort of thing a universal is; or, again, in terms of language, what it is that a general word is the name of, if it is the name of anything at all.

Now, in trying to discuss the problem of universals, one immediately runs into the initial difficulty, that we are using a number of technical terms, or pairs of correlative technical terms, which tend to be defined in terms of each other. For instance, what is a general word? Answer, a general word (examples 'table', 'monkey', 'docile', etc.) is a word which designates not a particular, but a characteristic or attribute of particulars, i.e. a universal. What is a universal? Answer 1, a universal is whatever is designated by a general word, such as 'table', 'monkey', 'docile', etc. Answer 2, a universal is whatever characterises, but is to be distinguished from, particulars. What is a particular? Answer, a particular is what has a specific date, or a specific date and place. But what does one mean by saying of something with a specific date and place that it is a particular? Not that it belongs to its specific date and place rather than to some other specific date and place, for if it did belong to the latter it would still be a particular. Then one means, by calling a thing a particular, that it belongs to some or other specific date and place. But what does not belong to some or other specific date and place? Answer, a universal.

The difficulty of avoiding such circularities has suggested to some philosophers that the reason why the problem of universals has not been satisfactorily solved even after two thousand years is that there is really no problem to solve; it has suggested to them that the whole discussion is a philosophical muddle which only needs to be shown to be a muddle to be dropped, in short that the best way to lay the ghost is to stop chasing it. As, however, I am not satisfied that the problem is simply a philosopher's muddle, and as in any case some understanding of the supposed muddle is necessary to an understanding of other topics in the theory of knowledge, I propose to discuss it briefly.

We may begin by putting forward as a provisional *description* of a universal that it is what is common to all objects which we normally call by the same name, e.g., whatever is common to all objects which we normally call by the name 'table'. That, it should be noted, is not offered as a *definition* of what a universal is. As a definition it could hardly be accepted without begging at least two major questions in the history of the subject: first, can there be a universal common to a group of objects, even if they have no common name? And secondly, can there be universals without instances? If our statement were taken as a definition, the answer to both questions would have to be No. But *prima facie* such an answer to the first question seems absurdly wrong, and although disagreement about a negative answer to the second question has been wider, yet it has, after all, been disagreement; it would hardly, therefore, be correct at this stage so to define a universal as to make such disagreement impossible.

All philosophers would, I think, accept it that there is something answering to the above description, and therefore that in that sense there are universals. For all that one is committed to, so far, in agreeing that there are universals is, first, that we do use words as general instead of inventing a proper name for each individual object, and, secondly, that there is something or other common to all objects to which we refer by the same general word. Where disagreement begins is at the next stage, at which we ask what *is* common to a group of particulars, or what is *meant* by the phrase 'common to a group of particulars'. The problem of universals is the problem of answering these questions.

## 3. Realist theories of universals

While they differed profoundly in their answer to the question what is common to a group of particulars, Plato and Aristotle did agree in certain respects, and may both be called Realists. According to

Plato, a universal is a substantive, an entity which not only does not depend on the mind for its existence, but does not require particulars either. It has its being in a non-temporal, non-spatial world quite independent of the world of space and time as we know it, and consequently although the existence of particulars in the latter does logically depend on the existence of universals in the former, the converse is not true; the universal Table would continue to be although all tables should disappear from our world and no table ever be thought of, let alone constructed, again. What, therefore, is common to a group of particulars called by the same name is that each of them stands in a certain (and identical) relationship to the same substantial entity or universal, the exact nature of the relationship being something which Plato never succeeded in explaining, even to his own satisfaction.

Aristotle, on the other hand, not only could not accept Plato's mysterious realm of substantive universals, but found it quite unnecessary. For him, a universal was not a substantive at all, but a characteristic or property. That is to say, it was essentially something which belonged to particulars, and was as logically dependent on them as they on it. Just as there could be no tables, unless the objects each possessed the characteristic of being a table, so there could be no such characteristic unless there were tables, real or imagined.

One might point the contrast between the two theories by saying that the appropriate part of speech to use for Plato's universals would be nouns, and the appropriate part of speech for Aristotle's would be adjectives. That would be far from giving the whole story, but it would be sufficient for our purposes. Now, although they differ on that point, whether a universal is an independent substance or a dependent property, they agree in being Realists, i.e. in holding that universals are what they are quite independent of the existence and nature of human or any other minds. If there were no minds, there could be no knowledge of universals, but to say that is very different from saying that if there were no minds there could be no universals to be known. Plato and Aristotle would agree both in accepting the first and in rejecting the second of those two hypothetical propositions.

They are agreed, too, on two further points of some relevance: first, that a general word is, strictly, a proper name; and secondly, that apprehending a universal is or involves an intellectual intuition of some kind. (By saying that they are agreed on those points I mean that their theories commit them to accepting those points, not necessarily that they explicitly said at any time that they did accept them.) A general word will be a proper name, because it is the name of one and only one thing, and because it stands in the same relationship to that thing as any person's proper name stands to him. We saw earlier that the word 'table' is unlike the name 'Montague Pinchington', because although the former is not the name of any particular spatio-temporal object, the latter is such a name. But, according to Plato's theory, although the word 'table' would not be the name of any particular spatio-temporal object, it would be the name of a single non-spatial, non-temporal object, namely, that entity by their relation to which all tables are tables. And, according to Aristotle's theory, although 'table' would be the name neither of any particular spatio-temporal object nor of a Platonic entity, it would be the name of a single feature shared by all tables. For each of them, then, 'table' is a proper name, private and personal, in the one case to a substance, in the other to a property.

Again, they would be agreed that awareness of universals is, or involves, an intellectual intuition, Plato because, in being aware of the universal Table, I am being acquainted with something which belongs to a world quite different from that in which my senses operate, and Aristotle because although by the aid of my senses I perceive this table, that table, and the other table, yet in being aware of them *as* tables (which is part of perceiving) I am doing more than accepting or recording sense impressions; I am noticing a single feature common and peculiar to each of these objects, and this noticing is an act of intellectual insight, of being acquainted with the universal Table.

### 4. Criticisms of Plato

What are the advantages and disadvantages of the two theories? Plato's theory was from the first subjected to a number of criticisms, by Plato himself and by Aristotle, into the details of which it is unnecessary to go here; most of them concern the relationship between the world of particulars and the world of universals, e.g. what exactly is or can be the relationship between any given table and the universal Table? More general difficulties concern (a) the intelligibility of the theory, and (b) the evidence for it. We are asked to believe in the existence of a world of entities quite distinct from the spatial and temporal world with which we are all familiar. It is easy enough to imagine such a world if we are allowed to think of it as a foreign country across the sea from ours, or as a world somewhere outside the planet on which we live, or outside the solar system within which our planet circulates. That is, I think, the way in which most of us persuade ourselves that we understand Plato's theory when we are first introduced to it and made to discuss it—as being something rather like but also very unlike the world with which we are already familiar. But, of course, such an approach is hopelessly illegitimate. This world of substantial entities exists, and is quite distinct from our own; but what do we mean by saying that it exists? or that it is separate from our world? We have got to mean by saying that it exists something totally unlike what we mean when we say of anything else that it exists. But how can we begin to do that, if the only meaning (or meanings) we have got for the word 'exists' is what we use when we say of anything belonging to our world that it exists? Can we, if we (as we should) insist on using words as having cash value and not simply as counters in a game or ritual, attach any meaning at all to the phrase 'timeless entity'?[1] Not only can I not understand what a timeless entity would be, but I find that however much I try to extend and torture the meanings of the two words I cannot interpret either in such a way that it can be combined with the other without self-contradiction. However, Plato's theory still has its defenders; I only wish I could understand what they are saying.

Difficulty (b) can be raised by asking the question, what reason can be offered why we should accept such a theory? No direct evidence is

1. Plato himself nowhere, I think, uses a Greek phrase of which 'timeless entity' would be a translation; and therefore, it might be said, this criticism hardly applies to him. However, he certainly thought universals were entities and that they were eternal. If by 'eternal' he meant 'lasting for ever', his theory is saved at least from the charge of self-contradiction.

or could be offered, no evidence, that is, which would take the form of producing a universal for inspection and showing that it is an object of just the kind which the theory said it was. Normally, when I say that something is an object of a certain sort and am asked to show that it is, I produce the thing, if I can find it, and display it to my doubter in a way which will reveal its character to him. e.g. I show that the cooked flesh of a turkey is white meat by producing a cooked turkey for inspection; I show that a piece of curtain material is not opaque, as the shopkeeper claims it is, by putting a light behind it and seeing the light through it; and so on. But no such method is available or ever has been, as far as I know, claimed to be available for showing that universals are timeless entities of the kind that they are according to Plato's theory. The only evidence for the theory would come from a transcendental argument, i.e. an argument of the form that although we do not know directly that there are such entities (as we can know directly that turkey's meat is white), yet we know indirectly that there must be, because otherwise our actual experience would not be of the kind that it is. Arguments of this kind, made more familiar by Kant, should always be approached with suspicion, because it is only too easy to invent a solution to a problem and yet to persuade oneself and others that one had not invented, but discovered it.

Supporters of Plato's theory are faced with the charge that it is not a theory backed up by any positive evidence at all, but an elaborate piece of mythology designed to fill a gap in a story; and I do not know what their answer would be. Certainly, our experience of the world and our use of language show that in some sense or other universals are necessary. But does it provide us with any reason for supposing that we are constantly having traffic with a mysterious world of eternal entities? It could, I think, only provide us with such a reason if it could first, and independently, show that all other accounts of universals are false. A liking for economy and for distinguishing theory from mythology should make us very cautious in reaching the conclusion that *all* other theories of universals are false.

One point that seems to have weighed very heavily with Plato in adopting his theory is that it makes it possible for there to be universals without any instances; and it must be admitted that it does make it possible. Plato believed not only that there might be such universals, but that there actually were, and that we knew that there were, notably the universals of mathematics and ethics. We know what a Euclidean triangle is, what it is for two figures to be equal in area, what a perfectly just action is; and yet we have never come across an instance of any of them. For the sides of any triangle drawn on paper or blackboard, however carefully they are drawn, can be shown by sufficiently close measurement to deviate in some degree or other from being perfectly straight; and its angles can be shown to add up to somewhat more or somewhat less than 180°. The supposed equality of two given areas is always only approximate, only accurate to a certain degree of error. And although we say of an action performed that it was the just (or the right or the good) thing to do, we can always imagine how it might have been somewhat better.

There, then, are three cases of universals, which appear to have no actual instances, but with which we are perfectly familiar. That there should be such universals presents no difficulties for a Platonic theory, according to which the existence of universals in their world is logically independent of the existence of particulars in *their* world. And to account for our knowing such universals Plato makes up a legend, that our learning by experience in our present life is really a matter of recollecting what we knew before our incarnation, and that given certain stimuli in experience, i.e. seeing roughly triangular diagrams drawn on paper, we are reminded of what we once knew but had until now forgotten, namely, the universal Triangle; similarly with Equality, Justice, and any other universals,[1] the apparent instances of which *are* only apparent, only approximations to instances.

Whether we need universals without instances, and how we could be aware of them, are questions which must be deferred. They are mentioned here because belief in the need for them seems strongly to have influenced Plato's general view of universals.

1. Indeed, according to one line of Platonic thought, the same account will have to be given of all universals, as none of them has instances which are more than approximate.

## 5. Criticisms of Aristotle

The Aristotelian theory, that a universal is a property simple or complex, common to a number of instances, has had on the whole a much stronger hold on philosophers, mainly, I think, because it seems so much more a commonsense theory. It does not require us to postulate the existence of entities for which we have no direct evidence, and it maintains that all that needs to be said about universals can be said wholly in terms of the world of our everyday experience. Few philosophers have not at some time or other found themselves attracted by it, because it seems, like so much that Aristotle has to say, so eminently sensible.[1] Nevertheless, I am doubtful whether it can be accepted as it stands, and that for two principal reasons.

The first of the two difficulties, like one of the puzzles over Plato, concerns the intelligibility of the theory. We are asked to suppose that there is something common to a number of instances, that this something is a feature or property, and we are to call this something a universal. We cannot reasonably object to the final request, if we can accept the first two suppositions. But can we accept them? What is meant by 'feature common to a number of instances'? In one sense, one has no difficulty whatever in answering that question. One can easily find, construct, or imagine situations in which we would normally say that a single feature was common to a number of instances, e.g. when we speak of a family nose appearing on several brothers or persisting through several generations, or when we say of two varieties of apple that, although they are unlike in almost every respect, they possess one feature in common, that they are good keepers. That is to say, we have an accepted use for a phrase such as 'feature common to a number of instances', and, broadly speaking, we can recognise cases where it would be applicable.

But this usage and this recognisability are the basic facts of the case, which a *theory* of universals must attempt to explain. If an Aristotelian theory is correct, it is so not because it allows us to have

1. Its most cogent advocate is perhaps Professor H. H. Price in his lecture *Thinking and Representation* (Proceedings of the British Academy, 1946), who argues more against its rivals than for it.

a usage for 'feature common to a number of instances', and to recognise cases of it, for in that it would not be distinguished from any other theory, but because it gives a satisfactory account of what it is for a feature to *be* common to a number of instances. It is when it goes to take this step, the step which marks it off from any other theory of universals, that I fail to understand what it is saying. There are various ways in which the notion of something being common to a number of other things or being shared by them can be understood, but none seems legitimate here. Two or more people huddling together for warmth can share the same rug, in the sense that they squeeze themselves or a part of themselves under a part of it; they can share the same fire, or the same room, or the same table, or the same bowl of soup, and so on; they can have a number of interests or maladies or friends in common, and so on. If one took just those examples alone and studied them, one would find a bewildering variety of senses of 'sharing' or 'having in common'. But what characterises them all is that what is said to be shared or had in common is itself as much a particular as the persons sharing it. Therefore none of these notions will serve to explain the Aristotelian notion of a feature being common to a number of instances, because in its case, although the instances are particular, the feature is expressly non-particular. And if we consequently exclude any usage in which what is common is a particular, I fail to see what meaning can be given to the phrase 'feature common to a number of instances', if we try to mean anything more by it than what was described in the previous paragraph.

If that is all we do mean it is unobjectionable, but it does not support (or count against) an Aristotelian theory of universals. All that we would then be meaning would be that a number of things were (to some degree or other) like each other; and that things are like or unlike each other is what we far more often do say than that they possess some feature or quality in common. But if we are to mean something more than that (and the theory's objections to a Similarity view of universals indicate, as we shall see, that something more is to be meant), and if we cannot follow any of the other usages of 'common' or 'being shared by', all of which are vitiated by what is common being as much a particular as are the things which have it in common, then an Aristotelian theory appears to be as unintelligible in its own direction as a Platonic theory is in its direction.

The second difficulty, perhaps, arises out of our inability to answer the first. If we try to imagine a universal which is exactly the same in each of its instances, so that they, as far as instantiating it is concerned, are different only numerically and not qualitatively, then it becomes hard to find many cases where a universal could plausibly be suggested to occur in this way. Certainly, we classify particulars, according as they resemble each other, or according as they have certain features in common (if that way of putting it is preferred), but how very seldom do the particulars which we classify together *exactly* resemble each other, and how seldom are they totally different from other particulars which we do not classify with them, and how often do we have to decide by decree or convention about borderline cases. An Aristotelian theory misleads, because it makes us think that objects can be parcelled off into neat and sharply divided compartments, according as each object possesses a certain characteristic or a certain other characteristic, because it suggests that the divisions between natural kinds are real and precise, and because it suggests that universals are things which we discover instead of being partly things which we invent. Zoologists, for instance, classify sea anemones as animal, although they grow as vegetables grow and have no power of locomotion; the flower known as sundew they class as vegetable, although, like the sea anemone, it catches its food (insects) by trapping; and there is a vast borderland of algae, which can be divided into animal and vegetable only by arbitration or convention.

Or let us take more familiar cases of artefacts, such as tables. Every reader of this book knows in the ordinary way what a table is (I am not referring at all to the multiplication tables, to tables for determining the date of Easter, etc.). What, then, is common to all tables? We might be inclined to answer that tables have in common two connected features, (*a*) that their top surface is flat and uniform, and (*b*) that they are used for putting things on. But just how flat and how uniform must the surface be for the object to be a table? When we go for a picnic and, finding a more or less flat-topped rock or tree-stump, say, 'Let's use this for a table', is it a table or is it not? How is one to decide such a question? Is it not a question of the sort that one decides not by discovering an answer but by choosing what shall be the answer, like the editor whose decision in a newspaper competition is final? We may decide to call it a table, because we think that someone deliberately put it there to be used as a table, or that however it came to be there and to have the shape it has it is frequently used as a table by picnic parties; or, as is more common, simply because it will serve us as a table on this occasion. As children, we are inclined to say, 'Let's pretend it's not a rock but a table' (as though it could not be both); as adults, having forgotten how to pretend, or not being sure of the borderline of pretending, we are inclined to say 'Let's use it as a table'.

The point is that we are not really unsure whether a certain universal is there or not. If we are unsure about anything at all, it is about degrees of likeness or unlikeness: as something to put plates on the rock is pretty good, for lemonade bottles or thermos flasks it may be all right if we choose our spots carefully, but as a surface for writing a letter on it would be useless. That is, there seem to be two sides to the matter: whether it is a table depends first on how far its dissimilarities go from what we would ordinarily call a table, and, secondly, on how far *we* are prepared to go before we say that the dissimilarities are too great for it to be called a table. Now, that is surely something much more like the editor's decision being final than looking for, and perhaps finding, something which was waiting there to be found all the time.

Again, what is the universal feature common to aeroplanes? If we are asked what an aeroplane is, we may start, say, by thinking of something like a Spitfire, or a Heinkel, or a Dakota, i.e. of something powered by an engine (or more than one) and controlled by a pilot. (We put in the engine to distinguish it from a glider.) But, of course, it does not have to be controlled by a pilot. For it can be controlled electrically by a man on the ground. Or, in that case, shall we decide to call him the pilot? We can or not, as we please; on the whole, we do not. It can still be an aeroplane, then, although there is nobody on board. Is it an aeroplane only if it can be controlled while in flight? or also if the controls are set before launching? We tend, at present, to say the first, but it appears to be a choice of convenience; for we no longer have the clear-cut distinction between the flying machine which carries its own source of power and a projected missile which does not; V1's, V2's, and other similar projectiles ended all that. If we called the latter not aeroplanes but flying bombs, it may have been because they were not controllable after launching, although more probably it was due to their being designed to explode on impact at the end of their flight (as though that prevented them from being aeroplanes). The glider bomb was controllable in flight, but was not called an aeroplane, again perhaps because it was intended to hit a target and, hitting it, to explode. As new flying machines come along, making further and further departures from the objects which the Wright brothers urged into the air, we have no real difficulty in accommodating them as aeroplanes or not as aeroplanes. We have no difficulty, because we are prepared to do what other people do, because if the designers, makers, and aeronautical correspondents (especially the latter) call them aeroplanes, then they are aeroplanes. Once more the editor's decision is final.

The matter seems to come to this, that we decide whether an object is of a certain sort, not by discovering whether it has a feature (or complex of features) exactly like a feature (or complex) possessed by certain other objects, but by discovering something vaguer, something that has been called a 'family likeness'. In general, we may take various specimens and treat them as standard objects, calling all objects that are more or less like them objects of the same sort. But we may and do vary the elasticity allowed in 'more or less like', and we may and do vary our standard objects. The standard aeroplane has long ceased to be a meccano-like biplane.

Nevertheless, it will be said, although this account may show that the classification of complex objects into natural or into artificial kinds is a much less neat and tidy business than could be wished, yet it does not dispose of an Aristotelian theory. For the difficulty itself allows that there are likenesses and unlikenesses; and how can any two objects be alike, however remotely, unless they are alike in some respect? We cannot regard similarity as a primitive fact, for it always depends on a feature common to the objects compared. True, we often enough assert similarity without specifying the respect, e.g., 'How like his mother he is'; but in such cases we are always talking elliptically, not specifying the respect because it is so obvious that we do not need to point it out, or because we are too lazy to point it out. We could, we think, point it out if challenged ('He has got the same *retroussé* nose'), just as we could, if we must, expand the elliptical statement, 'How tall your boy is', into 'How much taller your boy is than mine (or than most boys of his age, etc.).' Now, in general, it must be admitted, we do not think it sensible to say that two things are alike unless we are also prepared to indicate, however vaguely, the respect in which they are alike, although I am not sure that to such a general rule there are not exceptions: for instance, it seems possible to detect a similarity between two smells or two tastes, and yet to be quite incapable of answering the question in what way they are alike. But even if apparent exceptions can be brought into line, so that all similarities are similarities in a certain respect, that by itself will not establish an Aristotelian theory. It would bring us back once more against the question of intelligibility; for if the respect in which the objects are similar is a single feature common to them, we shall be none the wiser until we have discovered what it is for a feature to be common to them. I think that an analysis can be given, although not of an Aristotelian kind, but discussion of it must be deferred until later in the chapter.

## 6. No universals without instances

If an Aristotelian theory of universals is true, it would follow from its definition of a universal that there could be no universals without instances. And this has been alleged as an objection against the theory, on the ground that there clearly are such universals, e.g. those in which, as we saw earlier, Plato was most interested. Now, one could only refute that objection either by showing *a priori* that an Aristotelian theory must be true, and that therefore there could be no such universals, or by showing, with regard to any suggested universal, that it has instances. The former method is not open to me, and the latter would take far too long to work out here. I must therefore dogmatically record my belief that there are no universals

without instances,[1] and therefore that the supposition that there are
does not militate against an Aristotelian theory; and I shall illustrate
it by one example, the case of straightness.

Limitations of space insist on a very brief and summary illustration, although a really satisfactory account would require many
pages; for the word 'straight' appears to stand for a considerable
variety of related but distinguishable notions, some defined, some
undefined, such that no one account can be expected to cover them
all. Nevertheless, something prefatory may be said here, the relevant
sense of 'straight' being the sense in which we define a Euclidean
triangle as a three-sided plane figure, each of its sides being straight.
The only reason for suggesting that Straight is a universal without
instances is that whenever we examine an alleged instance of straightness carefully enough, we can find some flaw in it, so that we may no
longer say that the line is perfectly straight. A line drawn on paper
may look perfectly straight to the naked eye, but will be disclosed
as full of kinks and gaps by a sufficiently powerful magnifying glass.
Consequently, it seems that we have to say that, although there are
no perfectly straight lines anywhere, yet there must be a universal
Straight, because we have, in fact, a notion of it, which we use as
much in rejecting a line as not straight as we would if we could find
a line to be accepted as straight. Therefore, we shall have to admit
at least one universal without instances, an admission consistent
with a Platonic but not with an Aristotelian theory of universals.

Now, on that argument several comments may be made. First, it
calls for the obvious and frequently given answer, that our line did
*look* straight. Closer study with a more powerful lens revealed the
kinks, but did not alter the fact that it did look straight before, i.e.
that it did look exactly what a line would look like if it were straight,
however closely and minutely examined. In other words, the line
looking straight *is* epistemologically an instance of the universal
Straight, a fact which is not undone by the line under the magnifying
glass (which, in any case, looks vastly different from the line seen by
the naked eye) not looking straight.

This, in turn, raises the query whether the contrast between a line's
looking straight and its being straight is not in fact misleading. It

1. I am talking of simple characteristics only, not of complex.

certainly suggests that, quite apart from the shape a line looks to have there is also a shape which it has, and which may be quite different. But do we not mean by the shape which the line has the shape which it looks to have under certain specifiable conditions? We all know when we should say that the lines marking out a tennis court are straight and when they are not. Are we to say that no ploughman ever draws his furrows straight? True, what would satisfy us as tennis umpires or as judges in ploughing competitions would not pass our tests as inspectors of precision instruments. But that suggests that a line's being straight is relative to the purpose for which it is drawn and to the measurement used. If the edges of two surfaces have to be straight so that they will fit each other exactly and will slide against each other smoothly, then the margin of clearance which may be allowed between them will be smaller or greater according as the surfaces are, say, a piston and the wall of a cylinder in which it moves, or a sliding wooden panel in a wall and the groove in which it moves.

It appears that whether a line is straight depends on the standard of measurement with which we compare it, and that the notion of a line being straight without reference to any standard of measurement is an empty notion. Consequently, if to say that there are no perfectly straight lines is to say that there are no lines which are straight unless relative to an accepted standard, then we should agree. But we would not then be agreeing that straightness is a universal without instances: in the one sense (relative) straightness is a universal with instances, in the other suggested sense (absolute) straightness is not a universal at all, i.e. the word 'straight' stands for nothing.

## 7. Simlarity theories

Dissatisfaction with Realist theories of universals, both in their Platonic and in their Aristotelian form, led to the evolution of a radically different type of theory, according to which a universal is not an entity at all, whether substantival or adjectival. On this theory, of which there are several variations, a universal is defined in terms of particulars and of the relation of resemblance between them; it is thus more like Aristotle than Plato, in that a universal is essentially definable *only* in terms of particulars, and therefore could not be at all in the absence of instances, but it is unlike Aristotle in that it does not allow a universal to be a feature reproduced in a number of particulars, numerically identical in each of them. According to this theory, which may be labelled the Resemblance or Similarity theory, the qualities of any given object are as particular and localised as the object itself. If I have two billiard balls, of the same composition, size, and colour, one of them on the table in front of me, and the other on the mantelpiece behind me, then the redness and roundness of the one on the table are themselves on the table, and so are to be distinguished from the redness and round-ness of the other, which are behind me on the mantelpiece. That is, although there is one sense in which the redness of both balls is the same, there is another sense in which they are different: each red is private and peculiar to the particular billiard ball which it charac-terises; and the sense in which the redness of both balls is the same is better rendered by saying that the red of one is exactly like the red of the other.

## 8. Nominalism

It might be suggested that not all variations of the Resemblance theory would agree even over the short distance so far covered. The case of Nominalism might be urged, as certainly being a theory according to which universals are to be defined in terms of resem-blance, but requiring the particulars only to resemble each other in being called by the same name. But, as far as I am aware, this extreme form of Nominalism, according to which *all* that is common to a group of particulars (or the *only* respect in which they resemble each other) is their being called by the same name, has never been seriously held by anybody except Humpty Dumpty, and by him only over a very restricted range at any given time.

If all that is common, say, to the class of cows is their all being called by the name 'cow', then clearly whether any given object is to be called a cow will have to be decided either arbitrarily or conven-tionally. If my cow calves, its offspring become cows only if I call them cows, and impose my will on all who have occasion to call them anything at all, or if my farmhands, neighbours, etc., freely agree with me to call them cows; and the visiting townsman who, pointing at one of them, asks whether it is a cow or a bull, will not deserve my scorn for his ignorance of the facts of nature, but will have asked a perfectly sensible question. Now, of course, such a Nominalism has only to be stated for it to be seen to be far too silly a theory for anybody to hold. Deciding that a certain object is a cow is not at all like naming a baby or a ship. We may, indeed, when in doubt about an object, ask our question in the form, 'What sort of animal do you call that?'; we are just as likely to ask the question that way as in the form, 'What sort of animal is that?' But that does not support this Nominalism, because, having received the answer that it is an okapi, we should think it quite natural and sensible (but perhaps totally unnecessary) to say, as we point to a similar animal sharing the same enclosure, 'And that is an okapi, too'. If this form of Nominalism were true, that last remark, so far from being a statement of the obvious, would be a quite unwarrantable leap in the dark.

## 9. *Hobbes's Nominalism*

A milder form of Nominalism has been advanced, notably by that nowadays unduly neglected philosopher, Thomas Hobbes. He held that a group of particulars resembled each other in being called by the same name, but he also held—and this is the important point— that each of these particulars was called by the same name as the rest because it resembled the rest in some other way besides merely being called by the same name. 'A *man* denotes any one of a multitude of men, and a *philosopher* any one of many philosophers, by reason of their similitude.'[1] But if it is *this* similitude which constitutes each of these persons being a philosopher, and their similitude in being *called* philosopher is only derivative from that, why should Hobbes be ranked among the Nominalists? The answer is, I think, that he certainly does *say* that nothing is universal but a general word, or that nothing is common to a group of objects apart from their being called by the same name.[2] But in so saying (apart from our original difficulty about extreme Nominalism), he is failing to notice a

1. *Logic*, pt. I, ch. II.
2. ib. cf. *Leviathan*, ch. ·v, 'there being nothing in the world universal but names; for the things named are every one of them individual and singular.'

distinction about words which it has been left for modern logicians to make, viz. the distinction between 'type' and 'token'. Take the word 'red' as an example. If I assert that the word 'red' occurs ten times on this page, or that it has the same meaning wherever it occurs, or that it means the same as 'rouge' in French, I am referring to the type word 'red', distinguishing it from its different manifestations. If, on the other hand, in reading a book I came across the sentence, 'His red handkerchief hung down from his pocket', and if I said that in that sentence the word 'red' preceded the word 'handkerchief', I should be referring to the token word 'red', that is, to one of the particular occurrences of the type word 'red'. We do not normally bother to make the distinction, and equally readily say, 'I can see ten "reds" on this page' and 'I can see "red" ten times on this page'. However, as the distinction is of philosophical import- ance, we should realise that in the first of those two sentences I am referring to token words and in the second to a type word; and the last word in each of those two sentences is a token word 'page' (i.e. two token words altogether), each of them being a token of the one type word 'page'. Token and type are so related that successive tokens of the same type mean the same as each other; e.g. 'page' in the first sentence means the same as 'page' in the second sentence.

Now, because he failed to make the distinction, Hobbes did not see that the sense in which a name is common to a group of partic- ulars each of which is called by it is the type sense, and that each time any one of the group is named a different token is used. If he had made the distinction, he would have realised not only that a numerically different token is used each time, but also that tokens of a single type may vary qualitatively, too. The way 'cold' sounds if I say it when I have a cold is very different from the way it sounds when I have not, and both are different from the way 'cold' sounds when I am shivering with cold; my general pronunciation is very different from that of someone less impervious to the influence of the BBC, such as a true Cockney, or an Australian, or a New Yorker. And the way I write 'cold' varies slightly every time I write it; again, 'cold' is different from 'COLD', but both alike mean cold. Further, to suppose, as Hobbes seems to have supposed, that there is something literally common to and identical in every instance of a given word is not only to obliterate the type-token distinction, and to ignore the considerable qualitative variations in tokens of the same type, but it is also to reintroduce an Aristotelian theory, with its attendant difficulties, making the universal now not a single identical feature common to a number of instances, but a single identical name common to them.

If an Aristotelian theory is objectionable, it is not redeemed simply by substituting a name for a feature. That is to say, a Nominalist must explain what he means by saying that a single name is common to a group of particulars, i.e. that two tokens are tokens of the same type. And it seems that Hobbes would have to say the same thing about words as he already says about things, that there is a relation of similarity between this token 'cow' and that token 'cow', but not between either of them and this token 'horse', just as there is a relation of similarity between this cow and that cow, but not between either of them and this horse. What would be meant, then, by saying that a general word is a name common to a group of partic- ulars is that for each of them (and on each occasion that it is referred to) a similar token word is used. And the fundamental fact would still remain, as we saw in the first quotation from Hobbes, that similar tokens are used for objects only because the objects are, or are thought to be, similar. If universals cannot be defined in terms of resemblance between particulars, nothing at all can be done to save Hobbes's theory of common names; and if they can be so defined, his theory can still only be defended provided that a name's being common to a number of instances is analysed in the same kind of way as the universal's being common is analysed, viz. by way of resemblance.

Hobbes, therefore, stands or falls with the Resemblance theory as such, and so does the so-called school of British Empiricists in general, despite their individual variations. To say that there is a universal Red is to say that there are objects each of which is red, or which resemble each other in being red. And the theory will say, as we saw earlier in discussing Aristotle, that the question whether the two objects are instances of the same universal or have a property in common (whichever language we prefer to talk) is partly a

<br>90 <br>Theory of Knowledge

question about the objects apart from us, 'To what extent are they alike?' and partly a question about the objects in relation to us, 'Are they sufficiently alike for us to call them by the same name?' To what extent they are alike is for us to *discover*; and they will be to that extent alike, whether we discover it or not. That they are sufficiently alike for us to call them by the same name is for us to *decide*; and that our decisions will depend on our needs and interests is borne out by the fact that a dress designer or a painter would give two different names to the colours of two pieces of material, both of which I should call red.

## 10. General words are not proper names

The fundamental difference between the Resemblance theory and the Realist theories is that, while for the latter general words are proper names, for the former they are not. There is no one thing to which the word 'red'[1] stands as there is to which 'Ernest Bevin' stands or 'Westminster Cathedral' stands. 'Red' names the quality red in any red object, and 'table' names any table, but their naming them is not at all like 'Ernest Bevin' naming the individual who was Britain's Minister of Labour during World War II and who subsequently became Foreign Secretary. A proper name is no use if it does not serve to pick out an individual, and a general word is of little use if it serves only to pick out an individual. If I called every member of my pack of hounds Trusty, you could not tell which hound I was referring to if I said that Trusty had fallen sick.

On the Resemblance theory, a general word is the name of any one of a group of objects, not the name for a specified individual among them; thus, 'hound' is a general word, 'Trusty' is not. And the mistake, according to this theory, which so many philosophers have made is of supposing first that there must be some single thing which the general word names (i.e. that a general word is a proper name), and secondly that because a general word is applicable to a number of objects, each of these objects must somehow or other embody this thing. Once we take the first step we are committed to

1. Unless explicitly stated otherwise, I am using 'word' in the sense of 'type word'.

the second. But why, the theory asks, take the first step at all? What ground have we for treating a general word as if it were a proper name? Certainly there is something common to all red objects, and that is not merely their all being called red. What is common is that they are all red; and what is meant by saying that that is common to them is that they resemble each other in each being red, the resemblance being susceptible of degrees of variation. The Resemblance theory does not abolish universals, unless 'universal' is taken to be the name of an entity. It asserts, on the other hand, that what is meant by saying that there are universals is that objects can be classified into groups (a) according to their degrees of likeness and unlikeness, and (b) according to our decision where and how to limit membership of the group.

## 11. Resemblance and open classes

Believing that the Resemblance theory is substantially correct, I must mention the objections commonly levelled against it. They are stated[1] in Professor Price's lecture already referred to, *Thinking and Representation* (pp. 31–4), and are three in number.

First, it is argued that the theory, while it can allow us to think of 'closed classes', cannot accommodate 'open classes'. A closed class is a class consisting of a finite number of members, all of which could be enumerated by a roll-call or catalogue. Examples would be the books now on the top shelf of my bookcase, the kings of England from the Norman conquest to the death of Charles I, the soldiers decorated in World War I, the civilians killed in World War II. In each of these cases the number of members is definite and known or knowable, and in each case one could refer to the class either by a descriptive phrase such as those used above or by an enumeration of the members; in the last two cases the enumeration would be long and difficult, but it could be made.

An open class, on the other hand, is a class whose membership is not closed, e.g. chairs, oak trees, cigarette packets, red-nosed comedians, in fact almost any class one cares to mention. Even if

1. Not, of course, for the first time. They constantly recur in philosophical discussions of the subject, and are, for example, to be found in G. F. Stout's *Studies in Philosophy and Psychology*, pp. 387–8.

records had been compiled and kept up to date of the names of all red-nosed comedians who have lived hitherto, there may be others to come, as yet unborn; but there are no more civilians to come who can be placed in the class of civilians killed in World War II. Instead of saying, 'All kings of England from the Norman conquest to the death of Charles I visited Windsor', I could, if I wanted to, say, 'William I was king of England and visited Windsor; William II was king of England and visited Windsor. . . . Charles I was king of England and visited Windsor.' I can do the corresponding unpacking for 'All the books now on the top shelf of my bookcase are detective stories', but I cannot do it for 'All red-nosed comedians are unhappy men', 'All oak trees grow from acorns', etc. Yet we certainly make statements of that kind as much about open as about closed classes. But, says the critic, if the Resemblance theory is true, how can we? how can we think of open classes at all? That is, how can we give 'all' a meaning in cases where its meaning cannot be expressed by an exhaustive enumeration?

I could think of the class of all the books now on the top shelf of my bookcase, because that class simply consists of certain individual objects which I have observed, my copy of *Trent's Last Case*, my copy of *Gaudy Night* . . . my copy of *The Maltese Falcon*; I could think of each of these books in turn and notice a resemblance between any pair of them, that they are both books on the top shelf of my bookcase, and the further resemblance that they are both detective stories; and I could summarise each of these comparisons in the concept, 'all the books now on the top shelf of my bookcase', and again in the proposition, 'All the books now on the top shelf of my bookcase are detective stories'. I could compare any red-nosed comedians I have met or have heard of, and I could summarise these individual resemblances in the concept, 'all the red-nosed comedians I have met'. What I could not do would be to form the concept, 'all red-nosed comedians', or formulate (let alone assert or deny) the proposition, 'All red-nosed comedians are unhappy men'. I cannot do the latter, because there being red-nosed comedians of whom I have not heard and never shall hear I cannot think of the individual resemblances between them and each other, or between them and those of whom I have heard.

What this objection comes to, then, is that, on the Resemblance theory, I cannot form the concept, 'all $x$'s', unless all $x$'s are exhausted by a list of individual $x$'s whom I have observed (interpreting 'observed' very widely). It is an epistemological objection, for it argues not there could be no open classes, but that we could not think of them. But it is an objection the force of which against a Resemblance theory I am quite unable to see. It appears to assert that, if the theory were true, then whenever one thought of a class, or whenever one used the word 'all', one would always mean the same thing; but that it is obvious that we do not and therefore that the theory is false. The fact that the proposition expressed by the sentence, 'All the books now on the top shelf of my bookcase are detective stories', can be expressed by an enumerative set of singular sentences, '$A$ is a book on the top shelf . . . etc.,' but that the proposition expressed by the sentence, 'All red-nosed comedians are unhappy men', cannot be so expressed indicates that we are not using 'all' in the same way in both sentences. One may distinguish between the two senses by calling one the *collective* use and the other the *distributive* use; and in its distributive use 'all' = 'if any'. The objection is, then, asserting that, if a Resemblance theory is true, we cannot form the concept 'if anything is an $x$', or entertain the propositional form, 'If anything is an $x$ it is a $y$'.

But why not? Take, as an example, the concept of red, and my thinking, 'if anything is red'. What I would be thinking there would be, 'if anything has a red quality', and if I had to explain what I meant by that I should either do it by reminding my critic that he knew perfectly well how to use the word 'red' (i.e. what objects to apply it to), and that I was referring to anything that was, in the relevant way, like any of those objects, or by pointing out some red and some non-red objects and saying that I meant anything that resembled the red objects as they resembled each other and differed from the non-red objects as the red objects differed from them. In short, I should be aware of open classes by thinking of all objects (i.e. of any object) resembling a given object or objects in a given way. Unless there is a difficulty for the Resemblance theory about saying that objects resemble each other *in a given respect*, there seems no real difficulty about thinking of open classes.

## 12. Similarity can be fundamental

But, in fact, there is held to be a difficulty for the theory about similarity in a given respect; and this is the second objection commonly brought against it. It is argued that when we say of two things that they are similar or alike, we are talking elliptically, for although we may not mention it, we cannot think of two things as being alike without thinking of them as being alike in some respect, and indeed without thinking, however vaguely, of the respect in which they are alike. This was referred to earlier, and the point was admitted, although with some hesitation. It seems possible that there may be some confusion between (i) $A$ cannot be like $B$ without being alike in some respect; and (ii) One cannot think of $A$ as being like $B$ without thinking of them as being like in some respect (or even without thinking of the respect in which they are (or are thought to be) alike).

Now, there is a certain tendency to suppose that if (i) is true, (ii) must be true also. But (ii) does not in the least follow from (i) as a little thought will reveal.

However, even (i), if true, might be held to be an objection to a Resemblance (or Similarity) theory, on the ground that in admitting similarity always to be similarity in a certain respect one is admitting that there must be something common to any pair of objects between which similarity holds. But it would only be an objection if one was admitting that, apart from the relation of similarity uniting the two objects, there was a literally *identical* something common to both objects; then, indeed, one would be back in the arms of Aristotle or Plato. But are we compelled to admit that? Certainly, if $A$ is a red sphere and $B$ is a red cube, there is a respect in which they resemble each other, there is something common to them both. They resemble each other in respect of each being red; what is common to them both is that each of them is red. It may be necessary to distinguish between

(a) $A$ (which is red) is like $B$ (which is red),

and

(b) the red of $A$ is like the red of $B$.

We may be using 'like' in rather different sense in each of these two sentences—i.e. similarity between objects ($A$ and $B$) may be of a logically different type from similarity between their qualities (the red of *A* and the red of *B*). But the sense of each could only be indicated ostensively, that is, by indicating examples of it. What is meant by saying that there is something common to *A* and *B* in virtue of which they are alike is that the red of *A* is like (maybe exactly like) the red of *B*. The likeness between the red of *A* and the red of *B* is, I would suggest, a fundamental and not further analysable relation. One can say, if one likes, that in that case one is asserting an identity. There is no harm in that, as long as we are clear that what we mean is that one is exactly like the other. There is harm in it, if it leads us to think that what we mean in asserting an identity is like what we mean when we say of a man that he is the *same* man whom we ran into at Paddington this morning. Because the word 'identity' and its associates are liable to make us think that way, it is preferable to say not that the red of *A* is identical with the red of *B*, but that it is exactly like it.

### 13. *Similarity not a unique universal*

The third objection is also to be found in Professor Price's discussion, and at somewhat greater length in an earlier discussion by Bertrand Russell.[1] Briefly, it comes to this, that the theory must treat resemblance or similarity as itself a universal. 'It is something of which there are *many instances*. It is, of course, a universal of relation. Its instances are not individual objects *per se*, but complexes. But it is a universal, all the same. So the most that would have been achieved would be to reduce all other universals to this one relational universal.'[2]

Lord Russell argues in the same vein, referring to philosophers who want to 'get rid of' or 'to dispose of' universals, and maintaining that as we cannot get rid of the one universal, similarity, we may as well admit all the rest. But that is a tendentiously misleading way of putting it. Nobody is proposing, or could propose, the abolition or the expulsion of universals, in the sense in which one might propose abolishing the House of Lords or the death penalty, or expelling

1. *Inquiry into Meaning and Truth*, pp. 343–7; cf. his *Problems of Philosophy*, pp. 150–1.
2. Price, op. cit., p. 32.

undesirable aliens from the country. It is not even being denied that there are universals, in the sense that things belong to kinds, and that we think of them as belonging to kinds. What is being denied is that things belonging to kinds require further entities, either substantival or adjectival, beyond the things and the relations between them. And what is being proposed, if anything, is the abolition of the *word* 'universal', which, because it is a noun word, one is so liable to think must be the name of *things* of a certain sort, as most noun words are, e.g. 'camel', 'typewriter', and 'rhododendron'.

But to return to the objection itself. Similarity is held to be a universal in the traditional sense because, although we can define other universals in terms of it, we cannot define it in terms of itself, and therefore we cannot avoid treating it as a universal of which there are instances, i.e. as a realist universal either in the Aristotelian or in the Platonic sense. For instance, we can define the universal Table in terms of the similarity holding between tables, Red in terms of the similarity between red objects, and so on. But what happens with Similarity itself? We have a number of similarity relations holding between pairs of objects. What right have we to say that they *are* all similarity relations? If we try to treat them as we treated tables and reds, we shall be defining Similarity in terms of the similarity relations holding between similarity relations, and so on *ad infinitum*. The only way to avoid such a regress is to treat Similarity as a peculiar universal, of which all similarity relations are instances. But if we admit that there is even one universal of this type, what reason can we offer for denying that other universals are of the same type? If Similarity is a universal of which this and that similarity relations are instances, why object to Red being a universal of which this red object and that red object are instances? This, as Professor Price says, 'is a very notorious difficulty, and perhaps by much repetition it has become a bore. Yet I do not think it has ever been answered.' Lord Russell concludes, although admittedly with hesitation, 'that there are universals. . . . Similarity, at least, will have to be admitted; and in that case it seems hardly worth while to adopt elaborate devices for the exclusion of other universals.'

But what does this difficulty come to? That we cannot define

similarity in terms of itself, without involving ourselves in an unending regress. But is this not to confuse ourselves over the notion
of 'defining a universal'? What we are in fact interested in doing,
what we feel uncomfortable about if we fail to do, is to classify
particular objects into kinds; and that we do, as we have seen, by a
dual process of noticing similarities and of deciding that the similarities are sufficient for us to group the particulars between which
they hold into the same kind; we accordingly so classify them and
use the same general word to indicate particulars of that kind. We
can do exactly the same with similarity relations as we do with the
qualities of objects or with other relations. If we insist on calling
classifying in terms of similarity 'defining a universal', then clearly
we cannot define Similarity. But why does this involve us in a vicious
regress, requiring Similarity to be a universal in some *other* sense?
The criticism seems to assume the principle that if *A* is similar to *B*
and *B* is similar to *C*, then both similarities must be the same, and
consequently that both are instances of a universal Similarity. But
this is to take advantage of an ambiguity in 'same'. Suppose that *A*
is a blue object, *B* is a blue object, and *C* is a blue object, and suppose
that we are asked whether the similarity between *A* and *B* is the same
as the similarity between *B* and *C*. The answer is that according to
one usage of 'same' it is, according to another it may or may not
be. According to usage (i) we say of any blue objects that they are
all the same colour, and in saying that they are all the same colour
we are simply saying that they are all blue; and according to this
usage we would say that the similarity between *A* and *B* was the
same as the similarity between *B* and *C*. Usage (ii) provides for the
case where, say, *A* is indigo blue, *B* is navy blue, and *C* is azure
blue; in this case and following this usage we do not say that the
similarity between *A* and *B* is the same as the similarity between
*B* and *C*.[1]

In fact, the general question whether two similarities are the same
cannot be understood, let alone answered, until the usage according
to which 'same' is being employed is made clear. If we are employing
usage (i) then the similarity between *A* and *B* and the similarity

1. Both these usages should, of course, be distinguished from the usage
already referred to, when we ascribe identity to an individual.

D

between *B* and *C* must be the same; but all that is meant by saying that they are is that *A* and *B* and *C* are like each other in being blue; and therefore that the similarities are the same does not entail that they are *instances* of a universal Similarity. If we are employing usage (ii) the similarities are not the same; and that they are not the same also does not entail that they are instances of a universal Similarity. Certainly for *us* Similarity is the arch-universal; and what is meant by that is that, if we were not clever enough to detect any of the similarities which we do detect, we should have no general words at all. That is, words such as 'similarity', 'resemblance', 'identity', etc., are logically presupposed by words such as 'table', 'typewriter', 'kangaroo', etc., but the former are as much general words as the latter. If the world were exactly as it is now, except that there were no minds in it, then it would consist of objects between which various relations of resemblance and dissimilarity would hold. What reason have we for saying that the presence of minds makes Similarity a universal of a different type from what it would be in their absence?

# 5

## JUDGMENT

### 1. Are there propositions?

The preliminary discussion in Chapter 1 of the answer to the question, 'What are we aware of in knowing and believing?' served to bring out two points.[1] First, it showed that the answer to the question cannot be 'Facts', at any rate in the case of belief, because beliefs can be false as well as true. As we confine the name 'knowledge' to that form of cognition which is not false, and would withdraw it from any claimant that turns out to be false (e.g. 'I thought I knew what the answer was, but I admit now that I was wrong'), we may, if we like, say that what is present to the knowing mind is simply a fact. But we cannot say the same of the believing mind, for the believing mind is often in error, and yet a belief is none the less a belief for being false. Secondly, the discussion introduced things called propositions[2] to do the job in the case of belief which facts clearly cannot do. A *prima facie* case appeared for dualism, according to which the mind's objects are in some way intermediary between the mind and what it is judging or believing about. Next, a *prima facie* case appeared against dualism, which was worked out as a case against dualism in perception, illustrated by the example of Locke, and which proved sufficiently damaging to show that if epistemological dualism is tenable at all, it at least is not tenable in the ingenuous form put forward by Locke. What I now propose to do is

1. p. 26 seq.
2. p. 29.

to consider more closely the nature of judgment and the question of propositions, which were left rather summarily in mid-air at the end of the earlier discussion.

First, what according to the view in question are propositions? They are, apparently, timeless independent objects which the mind apprehends in acts of judging. They are to be distinguished from sentences, on the one hand, and from events on the other. The English sentence, 'George Berkeley was born in 1685 at Dysart, near Thomastown, in Co. Kilkenny', is different from the Italian sentence, 'Giorgio Berkeley nacque nel 1685 a Dysart presso Thomastown, nella contea di Kilkenny', but each is an accurate translation of the other. They are accurate translations because each in its own language asserts the same thing: an Englishman hearing the first would understand just what an Italian hearing the second would understand. This something else, the common thing asserted by the two different sentences, is the proposition that George Berkeley was born in 1685 at Dysart, near Thomastown in Co. Kilkenny, and is to be distinguished from either of them. Again, it is to be distinguished from the event which it purports to describe, and which in this case it accurately purports to describe. Berkeley *was* born in that year and at that place. But while the event had a particular location and a particular date, occurring in a particular house in Dysart on a particular day, the proposition describing it has not. Although it is sense to say that a certain event occurred on 12 March 1685, it is not sense to say the same thing of a proposition. A proposition, then, is different, on the one hand, from any of the variety of sentences, written or spoken, in which it may be expressed, and, on the other hand, from the events which it purports to describe, and which make it true or false.

It is not, of course, to be supposed that the theory makes the relation between the proposition and event as simple and straightforward as it is in the example about Berkeley. There, the proposition asserted the occurrence of an event, but not all propositions assert (or deny) the occurrence of events. Some assert the features an event will have *if* it occurs, or assert that *if* an event of one sort occurs, then an event of a second sort will occur; the propositions and laws of natural science are of this kind. Such propositions are not proved false by the non-occurrence of a suitable event, while propositions of the first kind are proved false in that way. If Berkeley was not born at Dysart in 1685, then the proposition asserting that he was is false. But the proposition expressed in the sentence, 'If you throw the baby out of the window he will fall to the ground,' is not proved false if you do not throw the baby out of the window; it is only proved false if you do throw him out of the window but he does not fall to the ground—i.e. if one event but not the other occurs of the pair which are asserted to occur in conjunction, if they occur at all.

## 2. Arguments for substantial propositions

The arguments for such a theory of propositions are many and seemingly attractive, all being alike in that they show that propositions of the kind postulated satisfy the conditions which it can be seen that any theory of judgment must satisfy if it is to be acceptable. First, the theory makes possible what may be called 'objective truths' (and correspondingly objective falsehoods), e.g. the truths of mathematics or of logic. We all suppose not only that $3 \times 4 = 7 + 5$, but also that that is an objective truth, i.e. that it was true before anybody believed it, and that it is still true at any time, even if at that time nobody happens to be thinking of it. We tend to distinguish (whether rightly or wrongly does not matter here) between 'permanent truths' and 'passing truths'; those actual names may not be exactly accurate, but they are sufficient for our purposes. A permanent truth will be one that is true at any time, regardless of date or place, and a passing truth will be one that is tied down either to a particular point or within a given range of space and time. While it is true at any time or anywhere that $3 \times 4 = 7 + 5$, and that if $A > B$ and $B > C$, then $A > C$, it is not true at any time or anywhere that there were six degrees of frost here last night.[1]

This first argument for the proposition theory is concerned only with the permanent truths, or what I called earlier 'objective truths'.

1. i.e. the sentence 'there were six degrees of frost here last night' does not regardless of time and place express a true proposition. If there were six degrees of frost here last night, then the proposition asserting that there were is true, and is true regardless of the time and place at which it is asserted. But the form of the sentence in which it is asserted does depend on them: if I want to-day to report last night's frost, I shall have to use the sentence, 'There were six degrees of frost

We suppose that such truths are independent of anyone's happening to think them, and that thinking them is a case of discovering something that is already there rather than of inventing or constructing something for ourselves. If there are these timeless independent propositions which the theory asserts, and with which the mind comes into contact in judging, then thinking the proposition that $3 \times 4 = 7 + 5$ will be a case of discovery or rediscovery, of finding something (in this case a *true* proposition) which is always there available for discovery or rediscovery, and which does not vanish when one ceases to think it. In short, the theory claims to account for the permanence and the stability which are the main feature of objective truths.

Secondly the proposition theory allows for what may be called the 'publicity' of our judgments, and for the possibility of communication by means of language. Conversation between two men is impossible unless they understand each other, and agreement is impossible unless, in addition to understanding each other, they are agreeing to the same thing; mistaken agreement occurs precisely when they think they are agreeing to the same thing but are not, probably because they are in some degree misunderstanding each other. I can only talk to my wife because, when I use a sentence, she understands what I mean; and her understanding what I mean consists not only in being able to manipulate English words according to the rules of English grammar, syntax, and idiom, but also in being able to interpret the results of the manipulation as symbols having significance. If speaking and hearing were mere manipulations of words in accordance with the rules, conversation would be like a rather disorderly and purposeless game of chess (which often enough it almost is when people are talking for the sake of talking). What is in addition necessary is that the words and sentences should stand for or symbolise something; what they stand for is what they mean, and what they mean is a proposition. Thus, if I say to my wife, 'The

last night'; and if I want to repeat it *to-morrow* I shall have to use the sentence, 'There were six degrees of frost the night before last.' Both sentences express the same proposition, which could be expressed in exactly the same verbal form on each occasion if the sentence dated the event by the calendar and not by relation to the time of speaking—i.e. 'There were six degrees of frost here on the night 15–16 February 1947.'

telephone is out of order,' what I say is intelligible to her, not only because we both can operate sentences in accordance with the rules of the English language, but also because the same proposition is present to each of us. Something must be common or public as between us, and that something, which is clearly the meaning of the sentence I uttered, is provided by the theory as a proposition.

Propositions, being independent of minds, are not private to any one mind; therefore, what I am thinking may also be thought by others besides myself; and if I express what I am thinking by uttering the sentence, 'The telephone is out of order', it is possible for someone hearing me, given a sufficient knowledge of English, to think exactly what I am thinking. The theory is not, of course, saying that when two persons are conversing there is no difference at all between their thoughts, that each is only thinking what the other is thinking. It does not have to say anything of the sort, but only that there must be a minimum of identity of thought for conversation to be possible. I may be thinking of the telephone's demise in terms of a broken relay switch in the automatic exchange or of a failure in the supply of current, and my wife may be thinking of it in terms of a faulty receiver or more vaguely of malice or incompetence on the part of the G.P.O.; but whatever things each of us is thinking that the other is not, there must be a certain residual identity, for, if there were not, my wife would be no more likely to reply, 'Well, have you told the supervisor about it?' than to say, 'We shall have to buy some more', or 'Lend me your cigarette lighter', or any other remark that has no relevance to disordered telephones.

Communication between minds by means of spoken or written language provides the most obvious case of something being common to them both, but it is not the only case. Two men may independently work on the same problem, and reach the same solution of it; their ways of tackling it may have been different, but their original question and their final answer are the same as each other's: this again, the theory says, is made easy if we realise that the proposition posing the problem that A started with is not just the twin of but literally the same as the proposition that B started with, and that A's solution is literally the same as B's. The well-trained readers of *The Daily Blast* who agree with their paper's explanation of the failure of the Anglo-Ruritanian trade talks are all accepting the same proposition; a second and contrary proposition is accepted by that other band of citizens who approvingly read *The Morning Coo.* In each case we have a number of minds all with (although perhaps in another sense all without) a single thought; in terms of the theory a single objective proposition is assented to by the individual members of each group.

The distinction which the theory draws between a proposition and the sentences by which from time to time it may be expressed allows for the neutrality of propositions between languages. The English and Italian sentences quoted earlier both assert the same proposition, which belongs to neither language, and which is not especially related to either language; there is no such thing as an English or an Italian proposition; there are only English or Italian sentences which may be more or less efficient ways of expressing the proposition in question. An Englishman uttering the English sentence is asserting the same proposition as an Italian uttering the Italian sentence; that neither knows the corresponding sentence in the other's language, nor would recognise it if he saw it, is quite irrelevant, for what they have in common is nothing essentially to do with a form of words at all, but a non-linguistic proposition.

Just as a proposition on this theory will be neutral as between persons (this is what is meant by speaking of its 'publicity') and as between different languages, so also it will be neutral as between dates. If yesterday I thought that Christmas Day was on a Tuesday last year, and if today I think it, too, the proposition which I am asserting or assenting to is in each case the same; that my first thought occurred on Saturday morning and that my second occurred on Sunday afternoon does not alter the fact that in both I thought the same thing, namely, what is expressed in the sentence, 'Christmas Day was on a Tuesday last year.'

Again, propositions will need to be neutral as between attitudes, for I can wonder whether something is the case, and later believe that it is, and what I now believe is what I previously wondered. The various mental attitudes—of entertaining (or considering), of wondering, doubting, believing, disbelieving, feeling certain, etc. —can all occur or be taken up in different orders on different occasions. I may, for instance, first believe that Christmas fell on a Tuesday last year, then, when my wife insists that it did not, wonder whether it did or not, then doubt it, because on other grounds I find my wife's memory more reliable than my own, then disbelieve it because I realise that Christmas Day falls on the same day of the week as the succeeding New Year's Day, and because I seem to remember the latter falling on a Wednesday, and finally be certain that it did not fall on a Tuesday because I have now found last year's calendar, which puts it on a Wednesday. Each successive attitude is a different attitude adopted towards the same thing, and that thing will be the single proposition which in turn I believe, wonder about, disbelieve, and finally convincedly reject. Any theory of judgment, to be acceptable, must allow for differences of attitude towards something in some sense common to them all; and this the theory in question does neatly enough by making this common factor a proposition independent of them all.

One final point should be mentioned in favour of the theory, that it allows for the incompatibility which occurs between men's beliefs when they disagree with each other. If I judge that it is ten o'clock and you judge that it is eleven o'clock, our beliefs are incompatible in the sense that at least one of them is wrong, whether the other is right or not; and if I judge that it is raining now and you judge that it is not, our beliefs are incompatible in that one of us is right and the other must be wrong. Now, if judging simply involved minds and facts, we should not get the incompatibility which we require. Facts clearly cannot be incompatible with each other: indeed, the most common way of showing a man that what he has asserted is false is to show that it is incompatible with some fact or other; but if facts could be incompatible with each other, such a method of refutation would not be valid.

If I maintain that the grass was cut yesterday afternoon, and you refute me by showing me that the grass is now two inches high, I must accept your refutation on the ground that what I maintained is incompatible with admitted fact: or, if I do not accept your refutation, it will be not because I maintain that facts can be incompatible, but because I maintain that there is really no incompatibility at all—the lawn mower may have been set very high, or its blades may have been blunt, or the grass may have been so well fed that it shot up during the night. Nobody, I think, would seriously want to argue that facts could be incompatible with each other, although there are many things which we *take* to be facts until we find them contradicting other facts.

The case of attitudes is rather different: we do speak of attitudes being incompatible with each other, and in so speaking we may mean one or other of two different things. Suppose, for simplicity, that each of the two incompatible attitudes belongs to a different person. Then, on the one hand, we may mean broadly that their tastes differ and that they feel violently about it—e.g. one may like the smell of incense, and the other cannot stand it; they may even plea for divorce in some countries on the ground of incompatibility of temperament or mental cruelty. But incompatibility of attitude of that kind is clearly not what we refer to when we say that my judgment that it is raining now is incompatible with your judgment that it is not. What is involved there is surely the other kind of incompatibility, the sense in which what I believe is what you disbelieve. Here our attitudes are different and incompatible, but in a different way from the former. By saying that they are incompatible we mean, not that our feelings or tastes are different, let alone that we feel violently about the difference, but that *what* each believes is incompatible with *what* the other believes, so that we cannot both be right.

In short, the incompatibility in question, which we elliptically refer to our attitudes, is not an incompatibility between our attitudes at all, but is one between the *objects* of our attitudes, and is precisely the incompatibility which we have already denied to facts. We therefore require something which can be the object of a belief, and which can be incompatible with facts, and not only with facts but also with other things of the same sort as itself. For if I believe that it is now ten o'clock and you believe that it is now eleven o'clock, our beliefs are mutually incompatible, whether or not both of them are incompatible with the facts, as they will be if it is actually twelve o'clock. That we have got to make some provision for incompatibility of this kind can hardly be disputed. What simpler provision can we make than by accepting once more the propositions offered by the theory? As facts cannot be incompatible, and as in the relevant sense mental attitudes are not incompatible, for the incompatibility refers not to them but to their objects, it is argued that we must accept propositions as the only things that will fill the bill.

## 3. Difficulties in the proposition theory

So much, then, for the case that what the mind has before it in judging are not facts but independent objects called propositions. The arguments in the theory's favour which we have outlined indicate a number of conditions which a satisfactory theory of judgment must fulfil, and purport to show how this theory does fulfil them. We do suppose that universal truths, such as those of mathematics and logic, have an objectivity independent of anyone's happening to think them. It must be possible for men to think the same things as each other, to communicate their thoughts in conversation, to think the same things irrespective of nationality or language, to think today what they thought yesterday, to reject or to accept what previously they believed or doubted, and finally to disagree with each other in a manner such that at least one of the disputants must be wrong.

All these things must be possible, because they actually occur, and we are all perfectly familiar with all of them. Consequently, no account of the nature of judgment can be accepted which is not consistent with them all; and the arguments for the propositional theory have consisted in giving a catalogue of the requirements and showing that each in turn is satisfied by the theory. Nevertheless, despite all these points in its favour, I am unable to accept it. For that a theory satisfies the required conditions does not conclusively establish its rightness; there may be other theories which also satisfy the same conditions; and there may be other conditions, not yet specified, which it fails to fulfil.

## 4. What would a proposition be?

The attractiveness of the propositional theory lay in its supplying *some thing* required by each of the conditions in the catalogue. A thing was needed which could be objectively true, which could be neutral (or public) as between minds, languages, dates, etc.; and the required thing was offered by the theory in the form of a proposition. But now what kind of a thing is such a proposition? So far, nothing whatever has been learned about it except that it is the missing piece which completes certain conditions. When we ask what a proposition is, according to the theory, we are offered a somewhat thin and cheerless answer. First, what kind of existence does it have? Clearly, it does not exist as a physical object does. To say that a physical object, e.g. this book, exists either means or involves that it is here for anyone who likes to pick up, to read, to throw away, that if I leave it lying on this table the next person to come across it will find it on this table rather than on that bookshelf, that unless it is burned by fire or damaged by water it will probably look much as it does now for a good many years yet, and so on. In short, we have to talk of a physical object's existence in terms of possible perceptions, of spatial locations, of dates, and periods in time.

If the distinction which is commonly drawn in theories of perception, and which was indicated at the beginning of this book,[1] between sense data and physical objects, is a sound distinction, the existence to be ascribed to the former is probably different from the existence to be ascribed to the latter. Putting it in a conveniently graphic if not wholly accurate way, a sense datum may be thought of as a very small slice of the history of a physical object. The elliptical appearance we are given as we look at the penny certainly exists; but we do not mean the same thing by saying that it exists as we mean when we say of the penny that it exists. Of the elliptical appearance we mean that it *occurs*, and we do not suppose that it continues when we look away, or when we change position, so as to see a somewhat different ellipse. However, whatever the differences of existence which we ascribe to physical objects and to their sensible appearances respectively, both seem totally unlike the existence that a proposition may be supposed to have according to the theory. Existence for physical objects and for sense data involves both time and space, but existence for propositions must involve neither. To ask where a proposition is is clearly a silly question, for a proposition is just not a thing of the sort that can be seen or touched, or that can have any spatial relations at all.

1. ch. 1, p. 20 seq.

Similarly, temporal questions about propositions are silly, for one of the great points about them, according to the theory, was that they were timeless. If a critic objects that we obviously do ask temporal questions about a proposition, such as asking when it will become true, the answer is that we are asking the question, not about the proposition, but about whatever it is that the proposition itself is a proposition about. Certainly, in an ordinary and legitimate sense of 'become true' a proposition can become true if, for instance, it is a proposition about the future, and when events turn out as predicted: 'It will rain tomorrow' becomes true tomorrow when it does rain. But that is only a shorthand way of saying that whether the proposition is true or not depends on what happens tomorrow. If it is going to rain tomorrow, then the proposition asserting that it will is true now; although we may not know until tomorrow's rain comes that it is true, our knowing that it is true is not to be confused with its being true.

We must distinguish between a proposition's having spatial or temporal reference and its being itself a spatial or temporal object, i.e. standing in spatial or temporal relations to other objects. Many propositions have some spatial reference or other (e.g. when I say that my house is on the north side of the street), and most have some temporal reference or other (e.g. when I say that my headache hurts less now than it did), but none is itself spatial or temporal. Nobody may have thought of the proposition that material bodies attract each other before Newton thought of it, but the proposition did not come into existence on the day on which he first thought of it.

If the existence of propositions is not the same as that of physical objects or their appearances, neither is it the same as that of mental states, and for one of the same pair of reasons, viz. that mental states belong to the temporal order. As regards space, it is almost as silly (*pace* the thoroughgoing materialist) to ask where is a given mental state as to ask where is a given proposition—not quite as silly, because my present desire to go to the movies is related to my body in a special way: it may have among its causes some condition of my body, it certainly can only be fulfilled if my body is taken to a cinema, and in any case it belongs to me rather than to anyone else. Nevertheless, we never do ask of a specifically mental state 'Where is it?' as we do ask it of a bodily state, or a sensation. We say, 'Show me where it hurts', or 'Whereabouts do you feel the pain?' but we do not say, 'Where is this desire of yours for a cigarette?' or 'Whereabouts is your belief that you've got a flat tyre?'[1] Nevertheless, mental states are things which occur in time and have dates, which come, go, and reappear. My desire to go to the cinema started I am not exactly sure when, but about ten minutes ago; I first believed that the earth's surface was curved when I saw ships at sea disappear below the horizon; I felt alarmed by the sight of the policeman who called at our house until he said he was collecting for the Discharged Prisoners' Fund; and so on.

When the theory says that propositions exist, or have existence independent of any particular mind, it is saying something quite unlike what we mean when we say of a person that he exists, or of a mental state or a physical object that it exists. It has being, but it is outside space and time. It is a queer substantial entity, totally unlike anything else one ever comes across. Here, at the risk of exposing my pedestrianism, I confess myself completely baffled: the metaphysical status which we are asked to recognise these propositions as having seems to be the same as that which Plato's Ideas have, and is to me equally unintelligible. Incomprehensibility may be due to a defect either in the theory or in the capacity of the person trying to understand it. I can only record that I do find the theory incomprehensible on this question of existence, and pass on to other difficulties. Fortunately, incomprehensibility can be a matter of degrees; for, if it were not, the difficulty of its incomprehensibility would prevent one from even thinking of other difficulties; and as long as one leaves the question of propositions' metaphysical status shadowy one can see other difficulties.

## 5. The hypothesis of propositions is unverifiable

The next difficulty is perhaps a variation of the first, but seems worth emphasising, for it brings out a new point. According to the theory,

---

1. There are, of course, idiomatic metaphors, such as 'Where is your resolution gone?' But they *are* metaphors, and the spatial words are not taken literally. The badly behaved child who is asked, 'Where are your manners?' would be ill-advised to answer that they could not be anywhere.

we assert the existence of these substantial propositions, not because we discover by some form of inspection that they exist, although we had never noticed them before, but because they are required as a condition of the possibility of making judgments, false as well as true. Now, such a method of argument *appears* unobjectionable in itself and to be an argument of the sort on which the natural sciences mainly rely. The scientist wants to account for a number and variety of observed happenings, and proceeds to do it by formulating an hypothesis, such that if the hypothesis is true things will happen in the way he has already observed them to happen.

That is only the first stage of scientific procedure, and would have little reliance placed on it by any worthwhile scientist until various further steps had been taken; he would want to find out whether there was more than one hypothesis that would cover his observed facts, i.e. whether they were susceptible of any possible alternative explanations; he would want to verify his hypothesis, either directly (where that could be done), or, more commonly, indirectly, by working out what other occurrences would have to take place under a specified set of conditions if the hypothesis were true, and then by carrying out an experiment under that set of conditions to determine whether the predicted occurrences do take place. If they do not, and if he is satisfied that the experiment has been properly carried out under the correct conditions and that his deductions from the hypothesis have been accurate, then he will reject the hypothesis; if he originally formulated two or more hypotheses that would cover his first set of observations, he will want to discriminate between them by following out the experimental method for each in turn, eliminating every alternative that yields predictions which the subsequent experiments fail to bear out; thus, by outright rejection or modification of hypotheses, he proceeds until he is left with the simplest and most general hypotheses that both will account for the previous observations and will be successfully borne out by subsequent experiments.

Reverting to the proposition theory, we find that the existence of these propositions is the hypothesis formulated to account for the facts of judgment. Is it put forward *as the only possible* hypothesis, as that which is necessarily entailed by the facts of judgment being what they are? If it is, then the secondary stage of scientific procedure is not required, and can serve no purpose. For if the facts of judgment are what they are, and if they cannot be what they are unless there are substantial propositions, then the theory of substantial propositions can need no further verification. But if the existence of substantial propositions really is entailed by the facts of judgment, i.e. if it really is the only possible hypothesis, then it is very odd that so many philosophers, men not without intellectual perspicacity or honesty, should have been unable to accept it.

Is it, then, on the other hand, a more modest claimant, *as at least one possible* explanation of the facts of judgment? The difficulty here is twofold. First, there seems to be no further way of verifying the hypothesis, i.e. no further set of possible facts which can be deduced from it, and which can then be checked by subsequent observation; in short, the theory is not in this way empirically verifiable or fruitful. Secondly, it is hard to avoid the suspicion that to postulate the existence of propositions is only in appearance and not in fact to suggest a hypothesis that will account for the facts of judgment. To explain: we should not suppose that a scientist had accounted for the solidification of water at freezing point if he said that it was because water became ice at that point, or because there was a certain property about water which caused it to solidify at that point. His first alleged reason is no reason at all, for it merely states that water solidifies at freezing point because it solidifies at freezing point. And his alternative explanation is no better because, although it does not repeat itself as the first does, it simply says that there is something or other about water that makes it solidify, without telling us what that something or other is. He has not accounted in any way for the occurrence, but has merely declared that there must be something to account for it; we are none the wiser. But if he tells us that the cause of water solidifying is the reduction of the random motion of molecules to a point at which it is overcome by the attraction forces between them, so that they change from the irregular pattern of a liquid or gas to the regular pattern of ice, then he has given us a scientific explanation; and if we are capable of following his explanation, we shall have obtained an answer to our question.

Now, does the postulation of substantial propositions do any more to account for the facts of judgment than (a) to say that there must be something or other to account for them; and (b) to suggest that the name to be given to this something should be 'proposition'? We are none the wiser, as mediaeval enquirers were none the wiser when they offered the sort of explanation which Molière parodies in *Le Malade Imaginaire*, when the would-be doctor says that opium induces sleep because it possesses a *vertus dormitiva*. Such qualities were commonly called 'occult qualities', and were very properly exploded by Descartes. I find it difficult to believe that substantial propositions are not correspondingly 'occult substances', and that we are not being asked to solve a problem in the theory of knowledge by taking refuge in a myth. If a proposition is a something-I-know-not-what required for judgment, we are deluding ourselves if we suppose that by postulating propositions we are solving any problem at all.

### 6. *An infinity of propositions would be needed*

Finally (not that there are not other objections, mostly connected with time, too elaborate to expound here), the thought of the number of such propositions that there will have to be may give us pause. If to make a judgment or to believe something requires a proposition before the mind to be judged or believed, then the realm of propositions will have to contain a vast array of propositions, to provide for every judgment that may be made. There will have to be a proposition corresponding to every different judgment that ever has been made, is being made, or will be made in the history of the universe; and unless every judgment is determined in accordance with a rigidly causal scheme, it would look as if the realm would have to include not only a proposition for each actual different judgment, but also a proposition for every *possible* different judgment. Not only will there be every possible true proposition, but also every possible false proposition—if, indeed, to say that means anything at all.

To every slight difference in judgment a correspondingly different proposition will be required; and there will be more or less vague propositions corresponding with the more or less vague judgments which we make. For instance, I may want to tell somebody the size of a full-grown foxhound; but it will not be enough that there should be one proposition recording it. For there is any number of descriptions which I may give, starting with the less exact and gradually approaching the more exact. Quite ignoring the false descriptions I might give, all of which have to be provided for, I might start by saying that a full-grown foxhound was somewhere in size between a guinea pig and a camel, and then go on, substituting of a guinea pig rabbit, cat, cocker spaniel, etc., and substituting for camel lion, foal, Great Dane, etc.; for every one of these most exact formulations another proposition will be required.

Again, we all know how easy it is, when two men are talking, especially on a fairly abstract subject, for one to say something which the other will understand in a slightly different way from what the speaker intended, not very different, perhaps, not enough to send the conversation off the rails, but enough to justify us in saying that the same sentence did not mean quite the same thing for each of them. Are we, then, to suppose that to each minute difference in interpretation there corresponds a minutely different proposition available in the realm of substantial propositions? Hitler's cries for *Lebensraum* would seem a farce compared with the needs of propositions. One more queer class might be mentioned, which would have to be admitted—logically impossible propositions: they must be allowed, because they are made use of in judgments, e.g. in the judgments that they are logically impossible, and because they are used as the premises in *reductio ad absurdum* arguments. Not only then should we have to provide for propositions which are in fact false, but also for propositions which could in no conceivable circumstances be true. Such a world seems to threaten not merely the understanding, but even sanity.

## 7. *Proposition as the meaning of a sentence*

Turning now to consider what better alternatives we can find in place of the previous theory, I find it necessary to continue speaking in terms of propositions, although in a different sense. If this seems confusing, I can only reply that there is no other word in common philosophical usage which will serve as a substitute, and that here after I propose to stick consistently to this second, more common, and less tendentious usage. Hitherto we have considered whether there are mind-independent substances available as objects of judgment; and the name given to these putative entities was 'propositions'. We have seen reason to believe them difficult to accept. In future I shall mean by a proposition 'the meaning of a sentence'.

The question, 'Are there propositions?' which, according to the previous usage, seemed to be an important metaphysical question asking about existence, now is very easily disposed of. For it is the same as the question, 'Do sentences have meanings?' to which the answer quite obviously is that they do. Not that they *all* do, for plenty of arrangements of words can be constructed into sentences according to the rules of grammar and syntax, which yet possess no descriptive meaning at all: e.g. the sentences, 'The square root of 3 is blue', 'Monkeys multiplied by grass snakes equal tuxedos', and other linguistically correct but gibberish sentences of that sort. But most of the sentences which most of the time most of us use have descriptive meaning of some sort; and that is what I now mean by 'proposition'.

It is convenient to have propositions in this sense because we do often, as philosophers, want to make two distinctions. First, we want to distinguish between a sentence and what it means: a sentence is a linguistically correct (correctness admittedly being a matter both of convention and of degree) form of words written or spoken, read or heard, but something is usually understood by the sentence, and that something is its meaning; as we have already seen, different sentences in the same or in different languages can possess the same meaning; and the same sentence in different contexts or to different people can possess different meanings, either because the sentence is vague or because it is ambiguous—e.g. 'The 9.50 is hardly late today' may not mean the same to a stranger as it does to one painfully familiar with that particular railway's habits; and because the same word (i.e. the same shape or sound) often has two quite unrelated meanings, puns are possible (e.g. 'Bear right in the middle of the town'). It is convenient to indicate the form of words or linguistic pattern by calling it a sentence, and to indicate what the sentence signifies or means by calling it a proposition.

Secondly, we want to distinguish between what a sentence means and the fact which makes it true or false. This may not be an ultimately tenable distinction—as we shall see later it is not—if it leads us to treat a proposition as a *thing* of one sort and a fact as a *thing* of another sort. But it is a common enough working distinction of reason, which has its uses, as long as we do not allow it to mislead us. We do not, on the whole, talk of a sentence being true or false, but rather of its being correct or incorrect, and of what the sentence asserts as being true or false. And we commonly use expressions such as, 'It is one thing to discover what he means, but quite another to discover whether what he means is true'.

## 8. Propositions not independent entities

If a proposition is what we mean when we talk or write, then a proposition is present to the mind when we think or judge. We may speak of entertaining a proposition—i.e. of considering a meaning as preliminary to accepting or rejecting it, to judging affirmatively or negatively. This is not to say that thinking must be done in sentences, although my own experience suggests to me that it is all done in symbols of some sort or other. But clearly thinking and judging are done with meanings, that is, with what will be meanings of sentences, or bits of sentences, if they are put into words at all.

The exact relation of thought to speech raises a number of difficult and interesting questions which we cannot pursue here. But they do seem to be very intimately connected, to such an extent that it is very hard to see how an animal having no power of speech could, for instance, wish that it could be moved from this field to the next in four days' time. In our present sense, then, propositions are necessary to judgment; and what we require to do is to give a satisfactory account of judgment, without introducing the hydra-headed entities of the previous theory. If we can produce an account by which propositions are mind-dependent although the elements of which they are composed are independent of mind, we may hope to avoid both the extravagant multiplication of entities of the substantial theory and the difficulties of simple dualism.

Such an account would be quite consistent with the conditions listed earlier. The need for objective truths does not in fact require objective propositions. For while it is true that the proposition '3 × 4 = 7 + 5' was true before anyone thought of it and does not cease to be true if at any time nobody happens to be thinking it, its objectivity is satisfied provided that if anybody at any time thinks it, then what he thinks is true. To say that it is an objective truth would be to say that, although the proposition itself is mind-dependent, i.e. requires some mind or other, yet its character of being true is not in any additional sense mind-dependent. I may choose whether or not to think the proposition, but if I do, then I think a proposition the truth of which is independent of me or of anybody else who may happen to think it; nothing that anyone can do will affect its character of being true.

Whether I make the radio programme on the Home Service audible or not does depend on me, for I shall not hear it unless I switch it on; what I hear when I switch it on does not depend on me, and there is nothing I can do to alter its character; I can switch off again, but that is all. In other words, although a thing may depend for its existence on something else, what character it will have if it exists does not necessarily depend on that other thing. A proposition may require a mind in order to be a proposition, but its truth-value need not depend on that or any other mind. Now, surely that is all that is required for objective truths, viz. that their truth should be independent of this, that, or the other mind. Similarly with the other conditions: a proposition could be mind-dependent and still neutral or public as between different minds, sentences, languages, dates, and mental attitudes; and two propositions do not have to be substantial entities in order to be logically incompatible with each other.

## 9. Judging a multiple relation

According to the substance theory which we have been considering, judging is a relation relating two terms, the mind on the one hand and the proposition on the other. The more naïve theory mentioned earlier,[1] by which what is present to the mind when it judges or thinks is a fact, also makes judging a dyadic relation, that is, a relation between two terms which in this case are mind and fact.

1. ch. 1, p. 26.

Both Dyadic Relation theories of judgment having come to grief, the proposition theory because it requires us to accept entities of very doubtful character, and the fact theory because it would not allow us to make the mistakes of judgment which we do make, we may now turn to a more promising theory of exactly the opposite sort, the Multiple Relation theory advocated by Bertrand Russell.[1]

According to the other theories a unity is presented to the mind in judgment, but according to this theory the unity of the objects of judgment is produced by the act or relation of judging itself. Consequently, if such a theory can be substantiated it has enormous advantages simply in terms of economy, apart from any other reasons: if a proposition is now constructed by the operation of judgment, we do not require to have the vast collection of propositions in stock which the other theory needed, but require only that the materials should previously exist, to be combined in whatever way is required.

### 10. What a multiple relation is

Before outlining the theory, a preliminary explanation of what a multiple relation is may be needed. A relation unites two or more terms and relates them in a certain order. In the following examples the italicised words symbolise the relation, the other words being the terms of the relation:

(a) The mouse *ran up* the clock.

(b) Brutus *killed* Caesar.

(c) America *won* the Wightman Cup *from* England.

(d) Oxford *is south* of Banbury.

(e) Jones *asked* his wife *to return* his book *to* the library.

(f) Brown *rode* a bicycle *from* Land's End *to* John o'Groats.

In the first pair of examples we have the simplest of all relations, that holding between two terms; in the second pair we have three terms (for although (d) appears from its verbal form to be a two-term relation, it requires as a third term one or other of the Poles), and in the third pair we have four terms. Running up requires one thing to do the running, and a second thing to be run up; winning from requires one thing to do the winning, a second thing to be won, and

1. *Problems of Philosophy*, ch. XII.

a third thing for it to be won from; asking the return of requires one thing to do the asking, a second thing to be asked, a third thing to be returned, and a fourth thing to which it is to be returned; and so on. Other sentences involving five or more terms to a relation can easily be constructed. What is, therefore, meant by calling judgment a multiple relation is that it is a relation involving a number of terms, the number varying from one judgment to another. Each of the examples above, when treated as an object of judgment, will, as we shall see, form part of a new relationship with two more terms in addition to those of the original example. Thus, my judging that the mouse ran up the clock will be a complex involving four terms, although the mouse's running up the clock is a complex involving only two.

The second feature of a relation which will become important for our purposes is what is known as its order or direction. Although the proposition, 'Brutus killed Caesar', has exactly the same terms and exactly the same relation as the proposition, 'Caesar killed Brutus', yet it is a different proposition, as anybody can clearly see. In each case the order of the terms between which the relation holds is different, and the meaning of the proposition as a whole becomes correspondingly different; another way of putting it would be to say that in the first case the direction of the relation killing is from Brutus to Caesar, and in the second case the relation is from Caesar to Brutus.

Similarly in all other cases of relations, with one type of exception, where the relation is one of equality, or identity, or difference. If John and Jane are exactly the same age as each other, the two sentences, 'John is the same age as Jane' and 'Jane is the same age as John', express the same proposition. Here whether I happen to think of John as being the same age as Jane, or of Jane as being the same age as John, the order in which the terms are related makes no difference to the meaning, i.e. does not produce a different proposition. In all other cases it does, even where terms and relation are the same and where the different propositions are true. For example, although it may be true both that Darby loves Joan and that Joan loves Darby, the two sentences 'Darby loves Joan' and 'Joan loves Darby' do not express the same proposition, for Darby's love for

Joan is a different fact from Joan's love for Darby. Once again the order in which the terms of the relation are arranged governs the meaning of the sentence, or the proposition which it expresses.

So with any other example that one cares to think of: to make money out of the three-card trick it is not enough to know that the cards are the Ace of Spades, the Two of Clubs, and the Two of Diamonds, and that one of them is between the other two; you need also to know or to judge correctly whether it is the Ace of Spades in the middle, and if not whether it is on the left or the right; if one gets the order of the terms wrong, one picks on the wrong proposition and loses money.

## 11. The multiple relation theory

According to Russell's theory judging is a multiple relation, one of the terms of which is the judging mind (called the subject), and all the others of which (called the objects) are the elements which go to make up what is judged, these elements being particulars and universals with which the mind is, or can be, directly acquainted. If we take his own example, Othello's judgment that Desdemona loves Cassio, we do not say that Othello's mind contemplates a single object, Desdemona's love for Cassio, for there is no such object, but we say, rather, that 'Desdemona and loving and Cassio must all be terms in the relation which subsists when Othello believes that Desdemona loves Cassio. . . . Thus, the actual occurrence, at the moment when Othello is entertaining his belief, is that the relation called "believing" is knitting together into one complex whole the four terms Othello, Desdemona, loving, and Cassio. What is called belief or judgment is nothing but this relation of believing or judging, which relates a mind to several things other than itself.'[1]

Once more, the order of the terms in the complex is vital, for although all the terms and the judging relation are the same, Othello's judgment that Desdemona loves Cassio is different (and false) from his judgment that Cassio loves Desdemona, which is different again (and true) from Cassio's judgment that Desdemona loves Othello, which is also true. A belief or a judgment is a complex unity brought about by the operation of judging, which is true if corresponding to

1. op, cit., pp. 196–7.

it there is another complex unity consisting of the objects of the judgment arranged in the order in which they are arranged in the judgment complex. 'Thus, e.g., if Othello believes *truly* that Desdemona loves Cassio, then there is a complex unity, "Desdemona's love for Cassio", which is composed exclusively of the *objects* of the belief, in the same order as they had in the belief, with the relation which was one of the objects occurring now as the cement that binds together the other objects of the belief. On the other hand, when a belief is *false*, there is no such complex unity composed only of the objects of the belief. If Othello believes *falsely* that Desdemona loves Cassio, then there is no such complex unity as "Desdemona's love for Cassio".'[1]

The theory, which should be clear enough, may then be summarised in the following three propositions:

1. Judging is a multiple relation which (i) requires as its constituents a judging mind (*subject*) and the elements of the proposition judged (*objects*); (ii) arranges them in a certain *order*.

2. The whole judgment is a complex unity, the terms being severally united by the relation of judging.

3. The judgment is true if there exists a complex unity corresponding to it—in the sense that what are the objects in the judgment complex exist as a unity on their own (and in the same order) outside the judgment complex.

## 12. *Criticism of the theory*

Now, this theory, like all others, has come in for a good deal of criticism,[2] much of which seems simply to miss the point or to suggest as necessary conditions conditions which do not appear to be necessary at all; therefore, that the theory fails to satisfy them marks no defect in it. In my view the theory is substantially correct (although perhaps insufficiently informative):[3] it has the merits of simplicity

1. ib., pp. 200–1.
2. cf. G. F. Stout, *Studies in Philosophy and Psychology*, XII.
3. It would need considerable expansion, beyond anything for which there is room here, to explain how it could accommodate hypothetical judgments, negative judgments, and judgments which are such that either the subject term does not exist (e.g. 'The Archbishop of Winchester is bald'), or, whether it exists or not, the judger is not acquainted with it (e.g. 'The last Tudor king of England

and economy, and it avoids the difficulties in which the theories mentioned earlier are entangled. I am inclined to doubt whether the theory of truth which Russell seems to think is implied by it, namely, the Correspondence Theory indicated in proposition 3 above, either is implied by it or is tenable, but discussion of that topic will be postponed until the next chapter.

  But connected with that is another point which has always caused trouble for the critics, namely, the differences which appear between the alleged pair of complexes (the judgment complex and the fact complex), in particular the different rôle which one of the elements plays in each. Suppose we take a simple two-term relational proposition (which we will assume to be true), and symbolise it as $A \; r \; B$, where $A$ and $B$ are the terms, $r$ is the relation between them, and the order in which the symbols are written down indicates the order of the terms or the direction of the relation—$A$ stands in relation $r$ to $B$. Now, if we make this proposition the object of a judgment, where $M$ is the subject or judging mind, and $j$ is the relation of judging, we have two complexes:

  (a) the judgment complex $M \; j \; A \; r \; B$;
  (b) the fact complex $A \; r \; B$.

And these two complexes are said to correspond because in each of them $A$ and $r$ and $B$ occur, and occur in the same order $A \; r \; B$. If the fact complex had been $B \; r \; A$, the two complexes would not have corresponded, and if $r$ had symbolised a relation such as 'is the father of' or 'defeated', etc., then the judgment complex would have been false. For, if $B$ had been the father of $A$, or if $B$ had defeated $A$, then the judgment that $A$ was the father of $B$, or that $A$ defeated $B$, would be false. Where $r$ symbolises a relation such as 'is the sister of', 'loves', etc., then if the fact complex had been $B \; r \; A$ the judgment complex $M \; j \; A \; r \; B$ would not have corresponded to it, but *might* still have been true. For when $B$ is the sister of $A$ or when $B$ loves $A$, $A$ may or may not be the sister of $B$, and $A$ may or may not love $B$. If in such a case the judgment complex $M \; j \; A \; r \; B$ had been true, it would have been true because, in addition to the fact $B \; r \; A$ there

had a beard'). Further, the notion of universals being (with particulars) the materials of judgment would need analysis in accordance with the view of universals outlined in the previous chapter.

was another fact $A$ $r$ $B$, and because the judgment corresponded with the latter fact. Considering our two complexes (a) and (b), and looking for the differences between them, we find the following:

(i) In (a) there are four terms ($M$, $A$, $r$, $B$,) and one relation ($j$). In (b) there are two terms ($A$ and $B$) and one relation ($r$);

(ii) In (a) $r$ is a term; in (b) it is a relation;

(iii) In (a) the order of $A$, $r$, and $B$ is determined by $j$; in (b) the order of $A$, $r$, and $B$ is determined by $r$.

Now how, it is asked, can the theory possibly claim, in the light of those differences, that there is a correspondence between the two complexes? more particularly, how can it claim a correspondence between $A$ $r$ $B$ as part of the judgment complex and $A$ $r$ $B$ as the whole of the fact complex? Russell does not explain what he means by 'correspondence', but he appears to mean that a true judgment corresponds to fact when the only difference between the judgment complex and the fact complex is the presence of the judging mind $M$ in the one and its absence from the other. But if that is what he means, he is certainly wrong, because although the difference is covered by (i) above, differences (ii) and (iii) still remain. The real difficulty is that $r$ performs a different function in each of the two complexes, being a term in one and a relation in the other; and it has consequently been argued that however the relation $j$ may unite the elements in the judgment complex the fact remains, as Russell admits, that it is $j$ which does it, not $r$, and that it is $j$ which relates $A$ to $r$ and $r$ to $B$. If that is so, $r$ in the judgment is not performing its function as a relation, with the consequence that the correspondence which we want between $A$ $r$ $B$ within the judgment and the fact $A$ $r$ $B$, in which $r$ does perform its function as a relation, does not exist.

As it stands, the theory does appear liable to that objection, which, however, can surely be met by what is either a reinterpretation (it may be what Russell intended) or a modification. If we distinguish between two phases of judgment, namely, entertainment and assertion (or denial), the difficulty can be made to disappear. At the stage of entertaining, if the mind has to combine the two terms $A$ and $B$ and the relation $r$, it can produce not more than two combinations, entertaining either $A$ $r$ $B$ or $B$ $r$ $A$; the remaining verbal combinations $A\,B\,r$, $r\,B\,A$, etc., represent no thinkable combinations, nothing which can be entertained. That is to say, at the entertaining stage $r$ must already be doing its job as a relation, restricting the possible propositions to $A\,r\,B$ and $B\,r\,A$, and already providing the propositions with their unity. Then, in the light of the evidence or prejudice, or whatever else induces one to make up one's mind, intervenes the second stage of asserting or denying the proposition entertained.

Such an account retains what is essential to the theory: it avoids substantial propositions and replaces them by their elements, viz. particulars and universals; it makes not only the occurrence of a proposition but also its unity dependent on the process of judging; and it does not alter the account of truth. It simply takes cognisance of the fact that one cannot think in terms of relations without thinking of them as relating the appropriate number of things (as one cannot think in terms of qualities without thinking of them as qualifying something), and of the consequential fact that although the unity of the proposition does depend on the mind in the sense that it is the mind which entertains or formulates, it does not depend on the mind in the sense that the mind can produce it how it likes. With a given relation and terms only certain unities are possible; within that field of selection the mind is free but not outside it, for what the mind shall entertain is to that extent conditioned by the relation which is to be the component of the proposition entertained.[1]

1 For a more detailed working out of this theory the reader is referred to the paper on 'Facts and Propositions' in F. P. Ramsey's *Foundations of Mathematics*.

# 6

## TRUTH AS CORRESPONDENCE

### 1. Theories of truth and common sense

For years now one of the bitterest and bloodiest battlegrounds of philosophical theories has been that on which the dispute between rival theories of truth has been fought. Sometimes it has been a three-cornered contest, but more commonly it settles down into a straight issue between the Correspondence and the Coherence theories. As the conclusion which I shall eventually suggest indicates, I am inclined to think that their battle is a case of Tweedledum *v.* Tweedledee, and to agree with Samuel Butler's dictum that 'truth should not be absolutely lost sight of, but it should not be talked about'. Nevertheless, as so many words have already been spilt on the subject, a book of this character must attempt some *résumé* of them, in order to give some idea what the issues are or have been thought to be.[1]

So far as the names themselves suggest anything, the Correspondence theory would seem so obviously correct that one could be pardoned for wondering how it could ever have been doubted. According to it, a judgment is correct or a proposition judged is true

1. From a wide choice of books discussing one or other or both of the two theories the following may be a useful selection—pro-Coherence: F. H. Bradley, *Principles of Logic. Essays on Truth and Reality, Appearance and Reality*, ch. xv and xxiv; H. H. Joachim, *Nature of Truth*; B. Blanshard, *Nature of Thought*, vol. ii, ch. xxv–xxvii; pro-Correspondence: B. Russell, *Problems of Philosophy*, ch. xii; C. D. Broad, *Examination of McTaggart's Philosophy*, vol. i, ch. iv; A. C. Ewing, *Idealism*, ch. v.

if there is a fact corresponding to it, false if there is not. According to the Coherence theory, the truth of a judgment consists in its coherence within a system of judgments. Common sense seems to support Correspondence, and would cite the usages of language as evidence that the view is widely, if not universally, held. We say that a man's belief is correct if it agrees, or conforms, or accords, or corresponds with the facts, all of the above being phrases suggesting that truth is (*a*) a relation of some kind between what a man judges, on the one hand, and the facts of the case, on the other; and (*b*) a relation of a special sort, which we try to indicate by using names such as 'agree', 'correspond', etc.

Now, if that were all that the Correspondence theory maintained (and it *is* about all that common sense maintains), there would indeed be little dispute; and in that form no Coherence supporter would, as far as I know, wish to dispute it. What he would rather be inclined to say, and here I should agree with him, would be that what has so far been put forward asserts so little that it does not constitute a theory at all, and that it does not support the Correspondence of the philosophers any more than it supports (or opposes) the Coherence of the philosophers. For what is being asserted in (*a*) is that whether a man's belief is true or not depends on something other than his believing it; from the fact that I believe that the front door is locked it does not follow that the front door *is* locked, i.e. it does not follow that my belief is true. In short, for a belief to be true or false there must be something else beyond that belief in virtue of which it is true or false. But, it may be objected, common sense does maintain more than that, for it supposes that the something more, in virtue of which a true belief is true and a false belief false, is a fact. So, indeed, it does, but so also, I think, do the Coherence supporters; none of them would be supposed to deny that, if my belief that the front door is locked is true, it is true because the front door is locked. What they would, however, say is that a fact is not quite the simple thing we are inclined unquestioningly to suppose, and that if we look into the matter we shall find ourselves driven to the philosophical theory of Coherence.

So far, then, there is nothing about the commonsense position to drive us into Correspondence rather than Coherence. We are all agreed that if a belief is true, it is true independently of its being believed, and that its truth depends on the facts. If we were disposed to ask no more questions, then we might be willing to be called Correspondence supporters. But the Correspondence which we should all then be supporting would be a very vague and unco-ordinated affair compared with the philosophical theory bearing that name; and unfortunately there are other questions to be asked.

As an instance of its vagueness the Coherence critic might point to (b) above, to the notion that the truth relation between a belief and what makes it true is a relation of a special sort which we indicate by names such as 'agree' or 'correspond'. That, too, he might admit, questioning, however, how much we have said that supports the Correspondence theory, when we have said that truth is a relation which we commonly indicate in English by names such as 'agree' and 'correspond'. For these words themselves are distres-singly vague or ambiguous or both. We say of two independently worked out solutions to a problem, that they agree, meaning that their conclusions are *identical*. We say that the results of a laboratory experiment agree with the hypothesis that we were testing, meaning that the actual results arrived at are those which were *deducible* from the hypothesis (plus the conditions setting the test). We say of the portions of a railway ticket torn into two that they agree, meaning that they *fit into* each other, as we say of a particular shoe found to fit a particular footprint that it agrees with it. We might, in any of those examples, have, without alteration of meaning, used instead of the word 'agree' the word 'correspond' (or 'tally', or a variety of others); but it would be difficult to maintain that in each of the examples the word 'agree' (or whatever substitute we might prefer) means exactly the same relation.

Again, many of the senses in which we use 'agree' conform more to the Coherence than to the Correspondence theory. This is particu-larly noticeable, perhaps, in the case of negation, where we reject a judgment as false when it is incompatible with something which we independently accept as true. If the results of our laboratory experi-ment are not what were to be deduced from our hypothesis, and if we are certain of the correctness of our conditions and calculations, we reject the hypothesis as being incompatible with our results. We may say of two beliefs that they do not agree, meaning thereby that they are mutually incompatible, that although they might both be false they certainly cannot both be true.

The upshot of this is that (*b*) offers nothing more positive in favour of Correspondence than (*a*) did, that we cannot argue simply from the fact that a label commonly given to the truth-relation is 'agree', 'correspond', etc. to the truth of the Correspondence as opposed to the Coherence theory. We may not do that because as often as not these labels (and their substitutes) in common usage have the meaning supported by the one theory *and* that supported by the other. Granted that the meaning of words is important evidence, which philosophers cannot afford to ignore, and which nowadays they especially emphasise, yet we must not cheat, either deliberately or through laziness, in the handling of the evidence: in this case we must not infer from the fact that the noises or marks used by common sense are the same as those used by the Correspondence theory that what they both mean by them is the same, even if we were prepared to admit (which many of us would not) that *if* they were the same the Correspondence theory must be correct.

In short, we must not be deceived by the sounds or appearances of words into supposing that what nobody would (I think) seriously dispute about truth makes Correspondence a foregone conclusion. The whole point is that what nobody would seriously dispute about truth is so little and so vague as to constitute almost nothing at all. To say that the truth of a belief depends not on the fact of its being believed but on the facts about which it is a belief no more settles the dispute between Correspondence and Coherence than to say the economic security of a country depends on avoiding a disequilibrium of imports and exports settles the dispute between the policies of high taxation, compulsory savings, or control of capital expenditure. The question in our case rather is: given that we all perfectly well understand what is meant by the statement that a belief is true (i.e. that we are in no danger of confusing it with other statements, such as that a belief is irrational, or that it is oldfashioned, or that it is held without great conviction, etc.), does a further analysis of the notion of truth enable us to say more about its nature than we have already as commonsense individuals asserted?

## 2. *Two questions to be distinguished*

To answer this question we may consider the rival theories in turn. And in considering them we need to distinguish two different questions, which when contrasted seem so obviously different that one could wonder how anyone could fail to keep them apart. Nevertheless, failure to attend to their distinction has certainly produced some of the misunderstanding by the supporters of one theory of the claims of another, and may even be mainly responsible for the evolution of the Pragmatist theory of truth, which under the patronage of William James has had such a long run in America. The two questions are:

 (i) What does the truth of a belief consist in?

 (ii) How can we test the claim of a belief to be true?

It may be that the answer to both questions is the same, that that which makes a true belief true is also that by means of which we discover it to be true; but we can hardly afford to prejudge the issue at the outset by assuming that the answer to both questions must be, or is always, the same. Clearly, if a satisfactory answer can be found to (i), i.e. if we can decide what the nature of truth is, then in any case in which we could discover that nature to be present we should have tested the claim of the belief concerned to be true.

In that sense an answer to (i) will also be an answer to (ii), but it will only be a *hypothetical* answer, saying that if, with regard to a particular belief, we can discover the presence of those characteristics which we found to be the answer to (i), we shall have proved that belief to be true. But such an hypothetical answer provides no guarantee that we ever shall discover in a particular belief the presence of the truth-characteristics; in practice, to determine whether a belief was true we might have to go about it another way, perhaps sometimes, perhaps often, perhaps always. For we must not make the further mistake, to which philosophers are prone, of supposing that there is only one answer to question (ii). There might be several ways of testing the truth of a belief, some more reliable than others, just as there are several ways of, say, testing the strength

E

of ice covering a pond, some more reliable than others. In a murder trial the discovery and interpretation of these clues may provide good reason for accepting the prosecution's claim as true, but they are not what we mean when we say it is true.

This seems to be the basic defect of the Pragmatist theory of truth, according to which a belief is true if it is useful, false if it is not, or more widely that a belief is true if 'it works'. Now that a belief is useful or works may be a very valuable criterion for testing its truth. But that it is useful is surely not what is meant by saying that it is true. For if it were what is meant, then the proposition 'That belief was false but it was useful' would be self-contradictory. Not only is it not self-contradictory, but one would have no difficulty in thinking of false beliefs which have been useful, and contrarily of useless beliefs which are true. Had Pragmatism maintained that the test of truth was a more important question than the nature of truth, it would have been on far firmer ground. It may be that question (i) is in the end not very interesting, and that the Pragmatist answer to question (ii) is both highly fruitful and consonant with scientific procedure. In that case the Pragmatist may say that he cannot be bothered with (i); but what he may not, and just what he does do, is to suppose that the answer which he offers for (ii) is really the answer for (i).

## 3. The terms of Correspondence

The first question that naturally falls to be asked about the Correspondence theory is what the terms are between which the relation of correspondence holds. So far, we have interpreted the theory as saying that it is a relation between a belief, on the one hand, and the facts of the case, on the other. Is it, then, to be a relation between one fact and another, the first always being a fact involving a belief or a judgment? For that I believe the sun is shining is just as good an objective fact as the fact that the sun is shining. The answer to this question is, I think, that we may say, if we like, that the correspondence is between the fact that I believe the sun is shining and the fact that the sun is shining, but that it is not a particularly helpful thing to say. It is not helpful, because it may disguise from our attention the element in the belief which is of primary relevance to the Correspondence theory—namely, *what* I believe. If correspondence is a relation between belief and fact, then that *I* believe that the sun is shining rather than that *you* believe it seems unimportant: which of us happens to hold the belief will not alter the relation of correspondence between belief and fact.

Again, it does not matter whether what I have so far called 'belief' is more determinately specified as 'settled conviction' or 'wavering opinion', or just plain 'hunch'; what sort of a believing it is makes no difference to whether the belief is true or not. Therefore, although it would on the Correspondence theory be in a perfectly good sense true that correspondence would be a relation between two facts, it would nevertheless be misleading so to describe it. The correspondence will be between what is believed and the fact of the sun shining; and following the procedure laid down in the last chapter, we may refer to what is believed by calling it a proposition.

That does not require us to hold that there are mysterious things, perceptible only to philosophers, called propositions; all it does is to call attention to the fact that whenever we believe we believe something, and that when we speak or write our sentences have (normally) a meaning. As the proposition that the sun is shining is that part of my belief that the sun is shining in virtue of which my belief (or the fact of it) could be said to correspond to the fact of the sun shining, I propose hereafter, in discussing the Correspondence theory, to speak of a proposition as being one term of the relation, as being that which is wanted to correspond with whatever makes the belief in question true. This, I think, is the normal procedure of Correspondence supporters, and it is also, I suspect, where they go wrong; but discussion of this suspicion must be deferred until the next chaper.

What of the other term, that in virtue of which a proposition is true? So far, it has been referred to as a fact, but that it is a fact has not yet been defended, nor, indeed, has fact been defined. Although I do not think 'fact' can be defined, yet what philosophers might call 'a definition in use' can perhaps be given, i.e. enough can be said about it to recognise what we are referring to when we refer to something as a fact; and it can best be indicated by contrasting it with an event. To say of *x* that it was an event is to say that it was a temporal occurrence. How long it lasts is quite unimportant, and whether we regard a temporal slice of history or a process as one event or as a sequence of events is purely conventional. We may equally say of an athletics meeting that it was the chief sporting event of the season, and of the hundred yards race at that meeting that it was the first event on the programme. In other words, where we make the cut between one event and the next, which parts of a process we think of as constituting one event is a matter for convention and interest to decide; the question, 'How long does an event last?' is as meaningless as the question, 'How wide is an angle?'

Nevertheless, the essential feature of an event is its having a date and possessing some duration; many events, too, have a spatial location, for many events involve material objects. It therefore makes sense to ask of any event, 'When did it happen?' and of some events, 'Where did it happen?' The way in which I am using 'fact' and in which it is commonly used is such that it does not make sense to ask of a fact, 'When did it happen?' or 'Where did it happen?' The dropping of the atom bomb on Hiroshima was an event which occurred in August 1945; there is a fact that an atom bomb was dropped on Hiroshima in August 1945, but the fact did not occur then. We use the various tenses (past, present, and future) of verbs to indicate the occurrence of events, but only the non-temporal present indicative of the verb 'to be' to indicate facts.[1] A fact in this respect is, as it were, an hypostasised event, an abstraction of what happened in an event. The actual event of the dropping of the bomb on Hiroshima was an enormously complicated occurrence, far too complicated to describe in even approximate detail; the fact is a conveniently intelligible aspect of the event, the way an event looks to a mind thinking about it.

Again, according to ordinary usage, an event is singular, which a fact need not be. The fact that an atom bomb was dropped on Hiroshima in August 1945 is singular in that it refers to what

1. An apparent exception, e.g. 'The fact that an atom bomb was dropped on Hiroshima accelerated the Japanese government's surrender' is only apparent. For it was not that fact which accelerated the surrender, but the Japanese rulers' realisation of it; and that realisation was itself an event or a complex of events.

happened at a particular place on a particular date; and if no bomb had been dropped on that place on that date there would be no such fact. But we also speak of general facts, such as natural laws of greater or narrower range. A man may be unaware of the fact that in England we drive on the left-hand side of the road; it is a commonly accepted fact that in a free economy increase in purchasing power is followed by increase in prices; no scientist will dispute the fact that water expands when it freezes; and so on. By saying that these are facts we are not referring to any particular event. Even though we may be referring to a *class* of events, it might be a class with no members. Scientists might have discovered the natural laws about the expansion of water, even though no water had ever frozen, and they certainly make use of laws about frictionless engines, even though no such engine has been, or will in the present causal system be, built.

We may further speak of universal and necessary facts, which are contrasted with those expressed in natural laws, because although the latter could conceivably have been different from what they are, the former could not. Although it is not the case that heated metals contract, it is conceivable that they should; we should be surprised, and maybe indignant, to discover tomorrow that they do, but we cannot know *a priori* that they will not. On the other hand that $2 + 3 = 5$, that if $A > B$ and $B > C$, then $A > C$, that whatever is coloured is extended are held to be necessary facts, which would apply not only in this but in any other conceivable world.

That explanation should suffice to show in what sense I am using 'facts', the sense in which, so far as I know, it is commonly used. I would not be thought to be committed to the view that there *are* facts in this sense, but it is necessary to talk as if there are in order even to begin discussing the Correspondence theory.

### 4. *Fact rather than event required as the second term*

What, then, is the second term of the correspondence relation—a fact or an event? The answer is not altogether easy, partly because supporters of the theory do not always make clear just what they mean by a fact, in particular whether they suppose there would be facts if there were no minds for there to be facts for. However, if we take the case of singular affirmative propositions (such as 'Mr Attlee broadcast on the Home Service radio at 9.15 p.m., 10 August 1947', 'Mr Winston Churchill died at his house in London on 11 August 1947', 'Gloucestershire beat Yorkshire at Bradford in 1947', etc.), it would seem plausible to say that the second term was an event.

In each case the proposition asserts the occurrence of a particular event, and the fact that in each successive case the dating of the event is less precise does not matter, for Mr Churchill's death could only occur once (so that as long as he died at his London house at any time on the day in question the proposition would be true), and Gloucestershire only played Yorkshire once at Bradford in the course of the 1947 cricket season. In each case, then, what would make the proposition true would be the occurrence of a particular event: in the first and third cases the proposition is true, for an event corresponding to it did occur—Mr Attlee did broadcast at that time, and the cricket match did end with that result; in the second case the proposition is false, because no event corresponding to it occurred—Mr Churchill did not die on that date at his house in London.

But the view that events are what correspond to true propositions seems much less plausible if we turn from the comparatively straight-forward case of singular affirmative propositions, asserting the occurrence of something, to more complicated cases. Take, for example, a negative proposition, such as 'Mr Churchill did not die on 11 August 1947'. That proposition is true, but to what event does it correspond? We would hardly say, unless we were struggling in the last ditch to save a theory, that there was an event consisting in Mr Churchill's not dying on that day.

At what time on that day did the event occur? We cannot say it occurred in the morning, for that would be consistent with his having died in the afternoon or evening, in which case the proposition would be false. We should have to say that the event of Mr Churchill's not dying on 11 August 1947 lasted all day; and although, as we have seen, there is no objection to saying that an event lasted all day, it does seem fantastic to suggest that if we are to give a complete account of Mr Churchill's life on that day we must include not only all the things which did happen to him, but also all the things that did not. What makes the proposition true is not the occurrence of an event to make it true, but the non-occurrence of an event (the death of Mr Churchill) to make it false; and the non-occurrence of an event is not an event but a fact, a queer sort of fact, perhaps, about the exact analysis of which logicians still puzzle themselves, but a fact just the same. We would say that it is a fact that Mr Churchill did not die on that day, or that as a matter of fact he did not die on that day, or that we know for a fact that he did not die on that day.

Similar difficulties break out over propositions which do not expressly refer to a given event at all, let alone assert whether it did or did not occur. First, *particular* propositions (propositions involving the notion of 'some') require, if they are affirmative, the occurrence of some events or the existence of some things of a certain sort, but the correspondence between proposition and events in this case does not seem to be at all like the correspondence in the case of *singular* affirmative propositions. The proposition, 'Some Englishmen went to Switzerland in 1947', is true provided that at least two Englishmen went there (interpreting 'some' as meaning 'more than one'); and in fact a great many more than two went, so that the proposition is true. But, although the necessary number of events occurred to make the proposition true, none of the events corresponds to it in the way in which events could be said to correspond to singular propositions. If Jones and Brown, who are English, went to Switzerland in 1947, the proposition, 'Jones and Brown went to Switzerland in 1947' is true, and so also is the proposition, 'Some Englishmen went to Switzerland in 1947', but clearly the two propositions are very different, and if we are to find something to correspond to the second as certain events might be said to correspond to the first, that something will not be an event or events, but a fact about events.

The notion of 'some' is rather like a blank cheque, the value of which is left unspecified and indeterminate by the man who made it out; and events are like the specific value which the payee of the cheque inserts. Events are hard, determinate things, with exact values, and there could be no such event as 'something-or-other happened', for something-or-other never happens; a perfectly determinate thing happens, which through ignorance or incuriosity we vaguely refer to as something-or-other. A feature of the events of 1947 is that more than one of them consisted of Englishmen going to Switzerland; yet this itself was not one of the events, but a fact about them.

Secondly, *general* propositions cannot plausibly be said to have events corresponding in at all the same way as singular affirmative propositions. A general proposition may be said to be, in the relevant sense, even further removed from events than particular propositions are, because it does not even assert the occurrence or existence of anything, let alone specify in the way that a singular proposition specifies it. What a general proposition does is to assert a connection of characteristics, without also asserting that anything exists possessing those characteristics;[1] and the nature of the connection will vary with the type of general proposition (matter-of-fact connection, formal implication, etc.). Examples: 'Water freezes at 32 degrees Fahrenheit', 'An Englishman is a hypocrite', '2 + 4 = 6'. What, if anything, could be said to correspond to the first example would be not a certain occurrence of water freezing at that temperature, or even a collection of such occurrences, however large it might be, but the non-occurrence of water remaining liquid when brought down to that temperature; and, as we saw earlier, non-occurrence is not itself an event, but a fact about events.

The proposition corresponding to a particular instance of water freezing at that temperature would be, 'This bowl of water was reduced in temperature to 32 degrees Fahrenheit, and at that temperature it froze'; and repetition of the event, i.e. the occurrence of other events like it in the relevant respects, would simply increase our collection of such propositions. But the proposition, 'Water freezes at 32 degrees Fahrenheit', is not merely a summary of such propositions, but asserts more, viz. that there are (i.e. have been, are, and will be) no cases of water not freezing at 32 degrees Fahren-

1. Some sentences in general form do express existential propositions, e.g. 'All buses stop here,' 'Nothing in the store over sixpence.' As these sentences are commonly used, they would be held to be false if there were no buses, or nothing in the store.

heit; and to that proposition no event, nor any series of events, corresponds. What, if anything, corresponds is a material fact about the constitution of water, such that *if* there is any water and *if* the water is subjected to certain conditions it will behave in a certain way.

In brief, then, whether or not Correspondence supporters say that singular affirmative propositions correspond, if true, to events, they will require facts rather than events for other propositions. For simplicity of exposition I therefore shall treat the theory as saying that truth is a relation of correspondence between propositions and facts, in the sense of each term which I have explained.

### 5. The relation of Correspondence

The next question which naturally falls to be considered is that of the nature of the relation of correspondence itself. As we have seen, merely to label the relation 'correspondence' does not tell us enough to warrant an opposition between the Correspondence and Coherence theories. Of the various accounts put forward I shall very briefly discuss five, which seem to be the most commonly advanced, viz. that the relation is:

  (i) that of copy to original;

  (ii) a one-to-one relation between the elements in each term;

  (iii) between two terms sharing a common structure;

  (iv) a combination of (ii) and (iii);

  (v) unique and unanalysable.

The first, the copy view, makes the proposition somehow or other mirror that which makes it true, and is clearly the simplest and neatest account: it would clearly be satisfactory to be able to say that a proposition was the mental reflection of reality, which is true when it is exactly like what it reflects, false when it is in some respect unlike; a true proposition would then be like the image of myself which I see in a smooth, flat, evenly backed mirror,[1] and a false proposition would be like the image which I see when I look into a defective or a distorting mirror.

To this account critics commonly produce a twofold objection, first that propositions are in general not in the least like the things

1. It is irrelevant here that a mirror reverses left and right.

they are about, and secondly that in particular there are degrees of exactness in the propositions which there are not in the things they are about. As an example of the first, the proposition, 'My dog is brown and lazy', is true if my dog is brown and lazy, but the proposition is not in the least like my brown lazy dog; it makes sense to say of that dog that it is brown or lazy or that it needs brushing, but it does not make sense to say any of those things of the proposition. Even in the case of the mirror image there are only certain very limited respects in which the image can resemble the original, and it would not make sense to say of a mirror image of my dog that it needs brushing; but in the case of a proposition are there any respects at all in which the proposition resembles the original?

Now, this objection, while it would be valid against a Correspondence theory which made the second term a thing or event, would not be as effective against the theory which made it a fact, for the fact of my brown dog's laziness is no more like my lazy brown dog than the proposition is. We should, of course, be using 'copy' in a very queer sense, because one thing is not normally said to be a copy of another unless both are visible, and although my dog is visible, neither the fact that it is lazy and brown nor the proposition asserting that it is are visible.

Nevertheless, if 'copy' was being used as a synonym for 'resemble', then that a proposition and a fact are invisible would not prevent them from resembling each other; for not only can other sensibles like two smells, or two sounds, or two tastes, resemble each other, but so also can insensibles, e.g. two arguments, or two religious doctrines. How far this answer would take the Correspondence supporter I am not sure, because unless he could maintain that the relation of resemblance was fundamental, he would need to specify the respect or respects in which the proposition and fact resembled each other; and that he might find hard to do, unless he made use of the accounts to be given under (ii), (iii), or (iv), in which case the so-called copy explanation would have been abandoned.

However, I cannot accept the copy theory of correspondence. As we have just seen, to avoid the objections brought against it, it has to reduce itself to one of the other views of the relation next to be considered. And more serious—to anticipate later discussion—I fail to see how a true proposition and a corresponding fact could resemble each other, because I quite fail to see what difference there would be between them. For two things to be qualitatively alike they must be numerically different, i.e. they must be *two* things; and I am unable to see that we require both facts and true propositions. But of that hereafter.

According to the second view of those listed above, the required relation of correspondence is what is known as a one-to-one relation between proposition and fact, i.e. to each element in one there is a corresponding element in the other. It might be illustrated by a school teacher calling the roll of his class and entering a tick against the name of each pupil who answered 'present', and a cross against the name of each who did not reply. Assuming that his roll is complete, and that no child present either fails to answer or answers for a child who is absent, the column of ticks and crosses will exactly correspond with the present state of the class, each tick representing one child present and each cross representing one child absent.

But, whether or not truth involves a one-to-one relation between the elements of the proposition and the elements of the fact, it cannot consist only of that, i.e. although a one-to-one relation were a necessary condition of a proposition being true it could not be a sufficient condition. For quite apart from the difficulty of elucidating the nature of the separate relations of correspondence between the parts which jointly constitute the correspondence between the wholes, there are two special difficulties.

(*a*) Reverting to the symbolism used earlier, $A$ and $B$ representing two terms and $r$ the relation between them, we should have to admit that there is a one-to-one relation between the proposition $A r B$ and the fact $B r A$; but we should not allow (save with certain special kinds of relation) that the proposition $A r B$ was true in virtue of the fact $B r A$, and we should have to say, with some relations, that the proposition $A r B$ was positively false in virtue of the fact $B r A$. Yet to each element in the proposition there is an element in the fact corresponding, and there are no elements in the fact left over with nothing in the proposition corresponding to them.

Compare, for instance, the proposition, 'William loves Mary', with the fact that Mary loves William; and again the proposition,

'Jack is older than Jill', with the fact that Jill is older than Jack. In each case there is for each element in the proposition a corresponding element in the fact, and *vice versa*. Yet in the case of the first pair, if the proposition, 'William loves Mary', is true at all, it is true not in virtue of the fact that Mary loves William but in virtue of the quite different fact that William loves Mary. And in the case of the second pair, not only is the proposition, 'Jack is older than Jill', not true in virtue of the fact that Jill is older than Jack, but it is positively false in virtue of that fact.

(*b*) Again, we might have a general proposition symbolised *aρβ* and a singular fact *A r B*, e.g. the proposition, 'all fathers have some attitude to their sons', and the fact that Mr Brown despairs of his son. There we have a one-to-one relation, in that to each element in proposition and fact there is a corresponding element in fact and proposition. And we should have another similar one, too, if there were, as there might be, another fact *C r D*, that Mr Thompson was very proud of his son. But we should not be prepared to say that the proposition, 'All fathers have some attitude to their sons', was true in virtue of Mr Brown's despair of his son or of Mr Thompson's pride in his. Once more, although a one-to-one relation may be necessary to a proposition being true, it clearly is not enough to constitute its truth.

View (iii), by which the correspondence is the unity of structure between proposition and fact, is faced with similar difficulties, and seems even less plausible. By unity of structure is meant that the formal pattern of the proposition is the same as that of the fact. But the pattern of the proposition, 'Abingdon is nearer the sea than Winchester is', is exactly the same as the pattern in any of the following facts: Southampton is nearer the sea than Newbury is; Edinburgh is nearer the North Pole than Paris is; the Prime Minister lives nearer to the Houses of Parliament than the Bishop of Birmingham does. That proposition and those facts all exhibit the same structure, but although in that sense the proposition corresponds to each of them, it is not true in virtue of any of them; and it is in fact false.

Nor will view (iv), which combines (ii) and (iii), fare any better, for although it escapes objection (*a*) to view (ii) it does not escape (*b*) nor the objection to view (iii) as it was stated above. Or again, in a rank of soldiers numbered off from the right, the proposition, 'No. 9 is next but one to No. 11', corresponds in the required sense to the fact that No. 3 is next but one to No. 5, but it certainly is not true in virtue of it; it would indeed be false if there were not a No. 11 or if there were a No. 11 but no No. 10 (i.e. if the rank were a rear rank and No. 10 were a blank file), for then No. 9 would be next to No. 11.

The inadequacy of all the above attempted accounts of the relation of correspondence should need no further belabouring here. They leave us with (v), the last of the suggested alternatives, that correspondence is a unique and unanalysable relation, which it is consequently futile to attempt to break down in any of the ways suggested by the other accounts.

Now this is in its way a dangerous argument. For although some qualities and relations must be unique and unanalysable, in order to provide the elementary constituents of more complex qualities and relations, it is abominably difficult to get agreement about any particular quality or relation whether *it* is unique and unanalysable. We can show it to be analysable, if we can produce an analysis of it such that the analysis of it fits all cases which it itself fits, and *vice versa*. But if any proffered analysis fails to satisfy that condition, we are left with the alternatives that (*a*) there is a correct analysis which we have not yet succeeded in hitting on; or (*b*) it is simple and unanalysable.

One would expect to recognise (*b*) to be the case simply by examining the quality or relation in question, and just seeing that it is unanalysable; and yet how hard does one have to look to see that? or how exactly does one recognise unanalysability? And in fact the supporters of the view that such and such a relation is unanalysable nearly always support it because their previous attempts to analyse it have failed; they therefore incur the suspicion that they are taking refuge from their earlier failures to make their theory good in a formula of mystery, not that it clearly *is* unanalysable, but that it obviously *must* be. But what this 'obviously must be' boils down to is that the relation obviously must be unanalysable if the theory is to be saved. Yet whether the theory is to be saved is precisely the main point at issue. I am not prepared to say that correspondence could not be a simple and unanalysable relation, but I find the method of discovery that it is of that character intellectually disquieting. It impresses me as being something of a dishonest solution, but I do not know how to argue further against it.

### 6. Objection considered that no judgments would be verifiable

The remaining objections to which the Correspondence theory is commonly subjected take the form not, as hitherto, of asking questions about the nature of the terms or of the relation itself, but of considering what the consequences would be if the theory were true. It is argued that if it were true we should never be able to verify any judgment at all, because the experience which is required to do the verifying itself involves judgments. That is, (i) we do verify some judgments by subsequent experience, (ii) experience itself is made up of judgments, (iii) therefore we can never reach facts of the sort required by the Correspondence theory, (iv) therefore, if the Correspondence theory is true, we cannot do what we know perfectly well that we actually do, namely, verify judgments, (v) therefore the Correspondence theory is false. Now, this argument can take one or more somewhat different forms, which can easily bamboozle the reader if he does not remember to keep distinct the two questions contrasted on p. 129. In this context they become:

   (i) Is Correspondence the nature of truth?

   (ii) Is Correspondence a (or the only) criterion of truth?

What this objection comes to is that we cannot use correspondence with fact as the test of a proposition's truth, because we can never get away from propositions to pure facts so as to make the necessary comparison between proposition and fact. But, even if we accept the premise of the objection, that all so-called observation of facts is itself propositional in form, the most it would prove is that Correspondence will not serve as a criterion of truth: it would not prove that truth is not Correspondence. This point appears to be more clearly realised by some of Correspondence's critics than others.[1]

No doubt, if the objection is sustained, it would show that the

1. e.g. Prof. Blanshard, op. cit. vol. II, pp. 228 seq., includes it in a chapter called 'The Tests of Truth'. Prof. Joachim, on the other hand, op. cit. pp. 19–24, makes the two questions run into each other in the most disturbing way.

claims of the Correspondence theory would have to be reduced to very modest and uninteresting proportions; and no doubt, too, most supporters of Correspondence have held that it provided not only the essence but also at least *a* criterion of truth. Nevertheless it has not been shown to follow from the fact (if it be a fact) that Correspondence does not provide an available criterion of truth that Correspondence is not what truth is; even as a criterion its deficiency would be not that it would not work even if we could use it, but that it is such that we could not use it.

## 7. *Premise of the objection; all experience is propositional*

Now let us turn to consider the premise of the objection, namely, that all experience is propositional in form, and let us take a particular illustration. Suppose that you have mislaid your book and I tell you that it is on the table in the next room; you walk into the next room, find your book where I said it was, and agree that I was right; by your action you have verified my judgment. These are, as it were, the documents in the case, which no theory of truth is going to dispute, although it may want them further elucidated. According to the Correspondence theory (in its straightforward form) I have asserted a proposition which you have verified by observing a corresponding fact. (That it was you who did the verifying rather than I is quite irrelevant, for I could have walked into the next room as easily as you.)

But, the critic objects, this is altogether too crude: we do not have purely mental propositions, on the one hand, and wholly non-mental facts, on the other, which if we happen to bump into them and to spot their correspondence with the mental propositions will enable us to verify the propositions; the dichotomy between propositions and reality is unfortunately not as sharp as that; in particular, observation of fact, which verification requires or consists in, is not simply a wide-eyed reception of something given. When you went into the next room and perceived the book on the table, you perceived it *as* a book (or even as *your* book) on the table, and in perceiving it as such you were doing a great deal more than merely registering what was sensibly presented to you. For you to have such an experience as perceiving a book on a table, you were drawing on your past in various ways. How could you think of the one as a book and the other as a table unless you have the concepts of each? and how did you acquire those concepts? Certainly not on this occasion, for the objects were not presented to you with, as it were, labels tied round them saying, 'I am a book' and 'I am a table'.

Thus, all so-called perception or observation is not simply the camera-eye recording the given, it is also the mind interpreting according to the pattern of one's past experience; and exactly what you will see will depend on what the pattern of your experience has been, in particular what your interests are, either in general or in this special case. In this instance you are much more likely to see the recognition marks by which the particular book you are looking for is to be identified, e.g. the small ink stain at the bottom of the spine, than if you had gone into the next room looking for the newspaper and had found it underneath the book. That is, a present perception is only intelligible in the light of one's previous experience, and is correspondingly itself a judgment, not an explicit judgment involving, say, the articulate sentence, 'This fits my concept of a book', but a sub-conscious ordering of the given within the scheme of one's experience.

Some might add, too, with Kant that in addition to the particular mental concepts drawn from past experience such as 'table' and 'book' one requires to make use of other more fundamental concepts, such as 'substance' (in the sense of 'thinghood') and 'cause', which are concepts not derived from experience but are somehow or other contributed to it, necessary conditions of the possibility of any experience like ours whatever. That is, in my perceptions I undoubtedly do see (taking sight as an example) things *as* things, I do see the book as one thing, the table as another, and both as different from the ashtray beside the book or the carpet on which the table stands. Now, although I may have learned empirically to distinguish books from ashtrays and tables from carpets, I could never do it unless I had the notion of thinghood independently. I could not ask myself the question, 'Where does this thing end and that thing begin?' unless I already thought in terms of things; and that anything is a *thing* is not information given to me by my senses.

Now, whether or not one agrees with the last point, that our perceptions require certain categorial concepts, not empirically acquired, nobody would, I think, care to dispute that our perception of the external world is built up out of our previous experience, or to maintain that what I see now is intelligible except as fitted into the pattern of what has gone before. A consequence of this will be that no perceptions are incorrigible: if all perception involves the conscious or subconscious use of memory, the classification of the present in the filing system of the past, there is no logical guarantee with regard to any given perception that one is not making a mistake, not mis-classifying. After all, we do make mistakes of just this kind, of thinking something is a horse when it is a mule, or that it is an oboe when it is actually a clarinet.

Many empiricist philosophers have been so alarmed at this jolt to their security that, although they have had to let the physical world totter in uncertainty, they have clung on to the sensible world and insisted that as long as we stick to reporting our sense-data we cannot be wrong. I can be wrong in supposing that what I see is a penny, but I cannot be wrong in supposing that what I sense is a brownish roundish patch. By throwing to the wolves what is admitted to extend beyond the immediately given, they think to save as certain their sense-data, because they are what is immediately given. This view, that I cannot make mistakes (other than linguistic) about the character of my sense-data, has enjoyed a long vogue, and possesses obvious attractions. But it appears to be of very doubtful validity.

Does sensing something as being a brownish roundish patch involve concepts or classification or memory any less than seeing something as a penny? True, the concepts involved may be far more elementary and less complex than most involved in the perception of material objects. But in the case of the latter, although the complexity of the concepts may aggravate the risk of error, the error is introduced by the conceptualising and classifying at all. There is therefore no reason to suppose that sensation, which certainly involves concepts of however primitive a sort, is in a peculiarly privileged position with regard to them. And have we not all had the experience of not being sure what a particular colour or smell or taste or sound is like? It is not merely that we are not sure what the smell comes from, or what the usual English name for smells of that kind is (although we can be unsure of both those things), but we are unsure about the smell itself—what exactly *is* it like? And if we can be unsure, why cannot we also make mistakes?

### 8. *Its relevance to the Correspondence theory*

Now how does all this affect the Correspondence theory? Remember that it is intended as an objection to Correspondence as a criterion of truth, to the view that we can verify a proposition by observing the corresponding fact, and by comparing the two detect a relation of correspondence between them. What we have admitted is that perception is, however inexplicitly, propositional; and the objection hammers this home as a nail into Correspondence's coffin by insisting that by observation we are not after all discovering a relation between a proposition and a fact, but a relation between one proposition and a system of others, namely, those to the pattern of which our present experience of observing belongs. In short, verification never consists in the comparing of a proposition with a fact or in discovering a relation between them; it must rather consist in the discovering of a relation between one proposition and a body of others, and this relation is, as we shall shortly see, the relation of Coherence.

### 9. *Not a valid objection*

This objection, which is so often treated as fatal to the view that correspondence can ever be used as a criterion of truth, seems to me to be of very doubtful value. In the first place it plays havoc with language, the sort of havoc which admittedly philosophers are peculiarly prone to play. For it in effect says that we cannot discover a proposition to be true by observing the facts, because we have just been shown that there is no such thing as observing the facts. What we always thought to be the observation of fact turns out, under scrutiny, not to be the observation of fact at all. We have all been suffering from a mass hallucination until the Coherence theory came along to rescue us from it.

Now such an argument really will not work. It is absurd to say that there is no such experience as observing the facts, when the phrase, 'observing the facts', is a phrase devised specially to name a certain kind of experience. It is as though a physicist, believing that objects are not coloured in themselves, were to say that there is no such experience as seeing colours. Maybe no physicist has ever said anything quite as silly as that, but they certainly have been known to say that the researches of microscopic physics show that we are quite wrong in saying that, e.g., a table is solid.[1] To deny that a table is solid because it is composed of electrons and protons in a high state of agitation is no sillier than to deny that there is such an experience as observation of fact because observation of fact involves some kind of judgment.

What the critic's argument has shown, if it has shown anything, is not that there is no such thing as observation of fact, but that it is perhaps a more complicated thing than the Correspondence supporters realised. But it does not show that they were *wrong* in saying that the truth of a proposition could be discovered by observing the facts and by detecting the correspondence between proposition and fact. It may be wondered, incidentally, how careful the argument has been to distinguish between perceiving an object (e.g. a book or a table) and observing a fact (the book being on the table). The supporter of the argument is very liable to say that from the fact that perception involves propositions it follows that there can be no observation of fact; but the one does not follow from the other at all.

## 10. Further objection rejected

The objection is sometimes reinforced by an argument that observations, however carefully made and thoroughly checked, are not accepted if they conflict with an existing body of scientific judgments,[2] e.g. miracles or the phenomena of psychical research. Therefore Correspondence cannot ever be an adequate criterion, for if it were we would not reject such observations. To this argument a number of replies can briefly be given. First, it would at the most show that sometimes (or perhaps often) we in fact do not use the criterion of correspondence, but it does not show what it should, that we ought not to use it. As the progress of science itself illustrates, the isolated

1. Contrast Eddington, *Nature of the Physical World*, p. 342, with Jeans, *Mysterious Universe*, p. 138.
2. cf. Blanshard, op. cit., pp. 235-7.

proposition which is in conflict with existing doctrine had turned out over and over again to be right, e.g. Galileo's *Eppur si muove*; that is, we have a number of well authenticated cases where the procedure of not using correspondence with observation as a criterion has been proved to be wrong.

Secondly, if we accepted the principle embodied in the objection, namely that no observational proposition is to be accepted if it conflicts with the existing body of judgments (if, indeed, there is only one such body), as a universal principle rather than as a cautionary maxim, we should be saddled with some queer consequences. If we saw some very surprising thing happen, which did not square with past experience, we should never accept it that we did see that thing until either we found a way of squaring it with past experience or other things like it began to occur so often as to outweigh in number and extent our previous experiences.

Now no doubt it is wise to be cautious about accepting surprising observations, but human knowledge would have made little enough progress if we had refused to accept any. Our hesitation in accepting a surprising observation is grounded in the lesson we have learned empirically, that *normally* things do behave in a coherent way and save us a deal of trouble by doing so. But when things persist in behaving abnormally we find the prop of coherence knocked away from under us and we rely on correspondence.

For instance, if the conjuror shows us an empty hat and then produces a white rabbit kicking and wriggling in his hand, we do not deny that it is a white rabbit. We may not have a clue where it came from, and we may believe that its appearance is somehow or other coherent with the established body of natural laws, but our belief in the observation is not based on that. It is in fact exactly the other way round: we think its appearance must be consistent with natural laws precisely because we accept the observation that it is a white rabbit. And finally, the strength of the body of propositions against which, if we are cautious, we normally measure our surprising observation resides in the fact that they themselves rest (or we believe that they rest) ultimately on observation.

We must conclude, therefore, that the Coherence arguments against correspondence as a criterion of truth are invalid. It must be admitted that correspondence cannot be the only criterion, for often enough it is not available. I do not say that the truth of the proposition, 'Richard III was a hunchback', is open to question because I never saw him. The truth of historical judgments is constantly being checked and confirmed or rejected, but not by the criterion of correspondence. However, this would only provide a serious difficulty for those supporters of the theory who argued that correspondence was the only criterion for determining the truth of a proposition; as far as I know, none of them has been so injudicious as to maintain that view.

# 7

## TRUTH AS COHERENCE, AND TRUTH AS FACT

### 1. Obscurity of the Coherence theory

The first and principal difficulty of the Coherence theory is to understand it. In its bare outlines it seems so wildly unplausible and to lead to such fantastic consequences as hardly to merit serious consideration. But to reject it out of hand would be unwise, for one would almost certainly be rejecting something most unlike the theory as held by its chief exponents, notably F. H. Bradley. The difficulty of understanding it derives from the fact that, far from being an isolated theory which can be taken or left on its own, it forms part of an idealist system of epistemology and of metaphysics, which is of a highly abstruse character, and which requires the utmost patience, not to say tolerance, in unravelling.

In the space available any attempt to explain such an interwoven system would be quite impossible, even if I were competent to undertake it. What follows, therefore, must necessarily be a simplified account of Coherence, made as little misleading as I know how, which may be sufficient to give some idea of its merits and demerits as a theory of truth. Readers who having tasted the ersatz product thereafter thirst for the pure milk of the word should turn to the authorities referred to at the beginning of the previous chapter.

A quotation from the most recent exposition of the theory may help to summarise the idealist view. 'That view is that reality is a system, completely ordered and fully intelligible, with which thought in its advance is more and more identifying itself. We may look at the growth of knowledge, individual or social, either as an attempt by our minds to return to union with things as they are in their ordered wholeness, or the affirmation through our minds of the ordered whole itself. And if we take this view, our notion of truth is marked out for us. Truth is the approximation of thought to reality. It is thought on its way home. Its measure is the distance thought has travelled, under guidance of its inner compass, towards that intelligible system which unites its ultimate object with its ultimate end. Hence at any given time the degree of truth in our experience as a whole is the degree of system it has achieved. The degree of truth of a particular proposition is to be judged in the firs' instance by its coherence with experience as a whole, ultimately by its coherence with that further whole, all-comprehensive and fully articulated, in which thought can come to rest.'[1] The aim of thought is to *identify* itself with the real, and knowledge would only be complete when it had become reality. Whatever that may mean, it may seem surprising that truth is to consist in coherence with a system, rather than in identification with the real which is coherent; but the former and not the latter is what the theory says.

Now what of this relation of coherence and its terms? About its terms no great difficulty is to be found: they are what we have been calling propositions. It is true that most exponents of the theory prefer to talk of judgments than of propositions, and that so to talk scarcely aids clarity. For by 'judgment' we commonly mean either or both (i) the act of judging, (ii) what is judged, and consequently in philosophical usage are liable to lapse into ambiguity. Nevertheless judgment in sense (ii) is what can be directly true or false, for even if truth and falsehood are sometimes attributed to judgment in sense (i), they are so attributed only in an elliptical way.

We may say, if we like, that a man's act of judging or asserting was false or wrong, or that his state of mind in so judging or asserting was false or erroneous, but what we mean by that must be that he was wrong in so far as what he judged, i.e. sense (ii), was false. The

---

1. Blanshard, op. cit., p. 264. The unclarity of the style is characteristic of the school and its air of penetrating the ineffable. This passage, however, is hardly characteristic of Professor Blanshard himself, who for the most part is the clearest writer to champion the idealist cause.

latter sense is therefore the primary sense, and to avoid ambiguity I shall use 'proposition' where I wish to refer to judgment in sense (ii). This usage need not involve perversion or mis-statement of the theory; for, as the final sentence of the passage quoted above indicates, its modern exponents are prepared to defend it in terms of propositions.

## 2. The relation of coherence

About the relation of coherence itself it is harder to be definite, partly because its various champions do not all speak with quite the same voice, and partly because it is represented as an ideal at which actually asserted propositions aim rather than a universal which the particular relations between propositions and reality instantiate or exemplify. Coherence in the ideal sense may, sufficiently for our purposes, be defined as the relationship holding between a body of propositions such that no one of them can be false if all the rest are true, and that no one of them is independent of the others. That is, between all of the several propositions there exists a mutual entailment such that any one of them is deducible from all the rest, and that no one of them could be true if any of the others were false.

Naturally the theory is unable to provide any actual example of such a coherent body, because *ex hypothesi*, being an unrealised ideal, there is no actual example available. But it could be illustrated by any familiar example of a rigidly deductive system, such as Euclid's geometry has been claimed to be. It might be said that within the framework provided by the postulates, axioms and definitions of that system all the rest is coherent: none of the theorems could be different from what it is the others remaining the same; and if any were missing it could be supplied from investigation of the rest. The system fails to furnish a perfect example of coherence, because the postulates, etc., require to be independently accepted; there is nothing about the system that requires us to accept them as true, and each is quite independent of the others.

Although it was not realised until the beginning of the nineteenth century that Euclidean geometry depended on a number of postulates, which we are free to deny or modify severally as we wish, the realisation has been fully exploited since in the alternative geometrical systems elaborated by Lobatchewsky, Riemann, Cayley, etc. Here then we have one of the approximate approaches to the coherence ideal; but because within each system the ends, as it were, are loose, because within each certain propositions can be true or false independent of certain others, the ideal of thoroughgoing reciprocal entailment is unattained, and alternative geometries are possible.

That example should provide a warning against one fallacious interpretation of coherence, into which one might find it easy to fall. One might be tempted to regard 'coherent' as a synonym of 'consistent'; and while in one sense of the latter it certainly is, in another very common sense it certainly is not. When we say of two propositions that they are consistent we very often mean that they are not incompatible, that they do not contradict each other, that they might for all that has been said both be true. For instance, if the police witness states that he saw the accused half a mile north of the scene of the theft ten minutes after it, and if a witness for the defence states that at the alleged time of the theft he was drinking with the accused in a bar a mile north of the scene of the theft, both statements are consistent. They might both be true, for it would not be physically difficult for the accused at one minute to be drinking in a bar and ten minutes later to be half a mile nearer the scene of the theft.

Any two propositions are in this sense consistent, provided that they are not contraries, i.e. provided that if one of them is true it does not follow that the other is false. If the police evidence had been that the accused was found at the scene of the theft less than two minutes after the theft, that would make it more difficult to accept both statements as consistent, although not impossible, for the distance could be covered by car in the time. But if the defence's evidence is that two minutes after the theft the accused was still in the bar, the two pieces of evidence now have become inconsistent: they may both be false, but they cannot both be true, i.e. if one witness is telling the truth the other is either lying or mistaken.

In that example the various pairs of propositions are related to each other in that each is relevant to a further proposition or (in this case) question, 'Could the accused have committed the theft?' But to be consistent, a pair of propositions need not be related in that way, for they may be wholly independent of each other. 'There goes Brown in his new car' is consistent with, e.g., 'Lord Mountbatten was the first Governor General of the Dominion of India', 'The tides are subject to the law of gravity,' 'The area of a circle is $2\pi r$'. If we accept it we are free to accept or reject any of the others (as we are likely to accept the first two and reject the last); and if we accept any of the others we are free to accept or reject it.

## 3. Coherence more than consistency

In that sense of 'consistent' 'coherent' does not mean 'consistent'. The postulates of Euclid are consistent with each other in that no two are mutually incompatible, but they are not coherent, as we have seen, in the way required by the theory. Naturally, if two propositions mutually entail each other, they are also not incompatible, and in the completed system of the ideal no two propositions could be not incompatible unless each was logically dependent on all the rest. But compatibility is a much looser relation than the coherence demanded by the theory and should not be confused with it.

If coherence is the relation of entailment which would hold throughout the completed system of knowledge, it follows that we cannot ever conclusively verify any given proposition by the test of strict coherence. For until the system is complete we cannot justifiably say that the relations of entailment which we think we have discovered are more than highly probable. But it would clearly be consistent with the theory to maintain that coherence as actually employed as a criterion of truth may be something less and looser than the strict coherence of the ideal. Some propositions we accept because we see them to be logically entailed by others which we independently accept, others because in the light of the evidential propositions they seem probable.

We talk of evidence itself 'hanging together', meaning thereby not merely that the several pieces of it are not positively inconsistent with each other, but also that taken jointly they make a reasonable story, such that if we accept one part of the evidence we would be justified in accepting it all. If the witness's statement that he was drinking with the accused in a bar a mile away from the scene of the theft at the time that it occurred fits in with the evidence of others present in the bar, and if we have no independent reasons for disbelieving their testimony, we accept it. If we accept it we should be on the whole disposed to reject the policeman's evidence that he saw the accused half a mile away from the scene of the theft two minutes later. We should reject it, not because it is logically excluded by accepting the defence's evidence, but because it is rendered improbable by it—in that sense the two pieces of evidence do not cohere; we should reject it with even more conviction if all investigation failed to produce any sign of a car having made that journey in those two minutes, or if the policeman claims not to have spoken to the accused at the place where he says he saw him but merely to have seen him across the road in the light of a street lamp.

With coherence in its narrower or wider sense as a criterion of truth few will want to quarrel. But that it is the only criterion is disputed. And even if it were the sole criterion that alone would not prove that truth *is* coherence. For coherence as the criterion of truth would be quite compatible with the view that truth *is* correspondence. We shall therefore confine discussion to coherence as the nature of truth and to the doctrine of Degrees of Truth.

## 4. Doctrine of Degrees of Truth

According to the latter, because the only fully coherent system of propositions would be the complete knowledge of all reality, any body of propositions or so-called knowledge that falls short of that will be only loosely coherent, and all propositions will be partly true and partly false; no proposition is wholly true and none is wholly false. Bradley indeed does something to palliate this *prima facie* surprising statement by distinguishing between the truth of certain fundamental principles, such as the coherence principle itself, and that of other propositions.

With regard to the first, he says of one such metaphysical principle: 'The Absolute really appears, but the conditions of its appearance are not known. Our former statement therefore is defective, and comes short of truth in the highest sense of that word. It needs correction somehow, but how to correct it we are unable to discover. Nor can we even take our statement to be in the end corrigible by any mere intelligence. Hence on the one side, because nothing intelligible can be set against it, its truth is ultimate and final; while on the other side that truth remains defective and must in a sense be called untrue. . . . All understanding and truth, upon my view, to reach its end passes beyond itself. It is perfect only when beyond itself in a fuller reality. But short of such a completion, and while truth remains mere truth, there are assertions which are so far ultimate and utterly true.'[1] There are then some propositions which are absolutely true, in that they are beyond corrigibility, although they are in some way inadequate—they do not say all there is to be said.

But the other class is more interesting because more startling. It includes not only the truths of observation but also those of mathematics,[2] which are both rated as finite truths, and are both intellectually corrigible. 'Every finite truth or fact to some extent must be unreal or false, and it is impossible in the end certainly to know of any how false it may be,'[3] their partial falsity being due to their being true only within certain conditions, which are not, however, stated nor even apprehended by the speaker of the truth. Thus although within the realm of pure mathematics we may have absolute truth and absolute error, because there we specify the conditions or at least assert that there are conditions, we have only relative corrigible truth if we try to state the truths of mathematics outside that science.[4] For instance, that $2 + 3 = 5$ I may accept as absolutely true provided that I interpret it simply as a formal proposition about the properties of number and order, but I may never justly claim to know its truth if I interpret it as a proposition of applied mathematics. All I can say there is (i) that it is partly true and partly false and (ii) that it is nearer to the truth than $2 + 3 = 6$.

Now surely there is a perfectly good sense in which '$2 + 3 = 5$', as a proposition about the world, is absolutely true, even although there may be other senses in which it might be false. It might be false to assert that whenever I have put two objects into a receptacle

1. *Essays on Truth and Reality*, pp. 272–3; cf. *Appearance and Reality*, p. 483.
2. *Appearance*, p. 478.
3. ib., p. 480.
4. *Essays*, p. 266.

and added three more I shall if I open the receptacle find five objects there. Not only might it be false to make such an assertion, but it very frequently is. After popping two sea lions into a tank and following them with three fish, one would be surprised to find anything more than the two sea lions on opening the tank; and even two white mice alone will rapidly add up to more than five, without the assistance of three others.

Nevertheless do I not, in the first case, know this to be absolutely true: that if I have put two objects (sea lions) into the tank and to them added three more objects (fishes) then I have put five objects into the tank? In that sense, is not '2 + 3 = 5' absolutely true? And is not the proposition, 'This page is entirely written in French', absolutely false? How can the Coherence theory deny that, or the doctrine of Degrees of Truth stand out against it? One is tempted to suppose that it is because the theory uses 'truth' in an esoteric sense, such that it includes not merely accuracy but also comprehensiveness. Yet is not this to confuse the question whether a proposition is wholly true with the question whether it is the whole truth? If to the enquiry by the badly injured victim of a motor smash, 'What has happened to me?' I reply, 'You have broken your leg,' my reply may be wholly true although I have not added, what would also be true, that not only is his leg broken but his foot has been severed from it at the ankle.

That 'This page is entirely written in French' is partly true would be argued on a certain analysis of that proposition such that it includes the less complex propositions, 'This page is written in some language or other' and 'There is such a language as French', both of which are true. Certainly they are true, and I should say, although the theory must deny it, absolutely and unconditionally true. But even if we accept that analysis, such that the proposition, 'This page is entirely written in French', does contain some truth, then (a) at least in its complete analysis we must be left with some component proposition which is absolutely and without redemption false; and (b) that a proposition shall contain some truth will be compatible with its being absolutely false. (a) would show that although most of our actual judgments may contain some truth it must be possible, if they are ever to contain any error, for some to contain no truth at all. And (b) would illustrate once more the peculiar sense the theory wishes to attach to 'true' and 'false'. That the proposition 'This page is entirely written in French' cannot be absolutely false unless this page has not been written on at all or does not exist, and unless coupled with that there is no such language as French, might be enough, one would think, to include it in the Raised Eyebrows Department; and some of us, it would seem in retrospect, were hardly justly beaten at school for not telling the truth.

## 5. Confusion in the doctrine

It may be argued, and has been argued, for the theory that because every true proposition logically depends on all other true propositions, no proposition can then be completely and absolutely true unless one knows all the others. But, even if we accept the doctrine of internal relations which is involved in that argument, the argument still seems to be sheer confusion. On the one hand, if it is intended as a statement about coherence as the *nature* of truth, then the question whether a proposition is true or not cannot depend on the question whether I or anybody else know the conditions on which it depends; a proposition does not gain in truth if I happen to know not merely what are the propositions which entail it but also that they themselves are true; and a proposition does not lose in truth if no evidence can be found for it whatever.

On the other hand, if the argument is intended as a statement about coherence as the *criterion* of truth, then although it does not lead to as fantastic consequences as the first alternative, it imposes a condition upon knowledge which there seems no valid reason for accepting: viz. that I cannot know a proposition to be true unless I know all the propositions which entail it. I have no doubt that among the propositions which entail '2 + 3 = 5' are many which I have never thought of nor am likely ever to think of. But not only does that reflection not weaken my confidence in the proposition, but also it suggests no reason why it should. May it be that the theory is confusing the notion of entailment with the notion of inclusion, and erroneously supposing that the missing propositions are inseparable from the meaning of '2 + 3 = 5'?

*6. Difficulties for Coherence; alternative sets of coherent propositions*

Finally it may be argued that the Coherence theory does not entail the doctrine of Degrees of Truth and therefore that even although the latter may be refuted the former could still stand. That one is not the corollary of the other I am, admittedly with hesitation, inclined to doubt. Nevertheless, even if they are separable, and the Coherence theory is left to stand on its own, it remains exposed to some formidable objections. The first and most obvious might be raised in the form of a question: what would be the position, according to the theory, if there were two (or more) alternative bodies of propositions, each set consisting of coherent propositions but itself inconsistent with any other set? Take, for instance, two alternative geometrical systems such as those of Euclid and Riemann. How should we tell by the coherence test which if either is true? and what would be meant by saying of either that it was true? To this difficulty the theory returns a twofold answer.

(*a*) If we are asking whether the coherence test will provide at any time an absolutely cast-iron means of deciding between two internally coherent but mutually inconsistent sets of beliefs, the answer is that it will not, nor has it ever professed that it could. At any particular stage, if we have to choose between two sets of beliefs we should choose in the light of the evidence, selecting the more coherent; but we must be ready to admit, on the revelation of further evidence, that the set which we formerly rejected is now more coherent than the one which we formerly accepted. That would have the consequence, not that our former decision was wrong at the time at which we made it, but that we would be wrong if we now stuck to it in the face of the new evidence. Similarly, if we had two contrary sets of beliefs with, as we say, nothing to choose between them, then we just cannot tell, in default of further evidence, which, if either, of them is true; if there really is nothing to choose between them, we should not choose at all, but if we must, then we may choose which we like, e.g. by tossing a coin, still being prepared to find afterwards that we made the wrong choice. This appears to be a wholly justifiable answer for the theory to make, if the objection is taken as a question about coherence as actually employed. There is no reason why, if the Coherence theory is correct, men should not go on making mistakes in their decisions or being in genuine doubt which decision to take, just as they do now.

(*b*) If the question is asking whether there could be two alternative sets of coherent propositions such that not only does each not fail in coherence now, but would not fail however many further propositions the evidence added, then the theory does seem to be in more serious difficulties. For suppose we had two sets of such propositions, the only difference between them being that each proposition in the one set was the contradictory of the corresponding proposition in the other, i.e. Set I consists of propositions *A B C D E* . . . etc., and Set II consists of not-*A* not-*B* not-*C* not-*D* not-*E* . . . etc. With two such sets we should never reach a stage where one was more coherent than the other, for the addition of any proposition to the one would involve the addition of the contradictory proposition to the other; and as one developed so would the other.

Now this objection cannot be laughed out of court as silly. If it sounds silly to suggest that two sets of beliefs might be held such that there would never be any way of choosing between them, it is because, as far as we know, that does not happen; what in fact happens quite commonly is the situation dealt with under (*a*). Nevertheless, this answer is insufficient, for it is logically possible that there might be two such sets of propositions; and if they are logically possible, so also must be their logical consequences. Now, the first consequence would be that in such a world either no propositions would be true or all propositions would be true, according to the exact formulation of the theory. If our theory was that that proposition was true which belonged to the largest set of propositions between which the relationship of mutual entailment holds, then no proposition would be true; for if the two sets each contain an equal number, which *ex hypothesi* they must, then there is no largest set, and therefore as no proposition in either set belongs to the largest set no proposition is true.

Alternatively, if the theory was of the form which we have previously assumed, that a proposition is true if it belongs to a set of propositions such that when the set is completed the relation of mutual entailment holds between them, then all propositions would be true; for every single proposition, whether it is *A* or not-*A*, B or not-*B*, etc., does belong to a set of propositions fulfilling that condition, and therefore every single proposition would be true. Consequently, we should have to hold, according to our version of the theory, that if the theory is correct, then either all propositions might be true or all might be false; and that it is our very good fortune not to have had that happen to us, so far as we know, in this particular world. Secondly, we should have to allow that of a pair of contradictory propositions either neither member was true or both were true, again according to which version of the theory we adopted. But in what world could it occur that if I held up a disc and said, 'This disc is red all over', and added, 'It is not the case that this disc is red all over', either neither or both my statements would be true? Either a disc is red all over, or it is not red all over; if there is a sense in which '$2 + 3 = 5$' is true, then in that sense it cannot also at the same time be true that '$2 + 3 = 5$' is false.[1]

Now the theory has an answer to this difficulty, but an answer which seems fatal to the theory itself. The theory 'does not hold that any and every system is true, no matter how abstract and limited; it holds that one system only is true, namely, the system in which everything *real and possible* is coherently included. How one can find in this the notion that a system would still give truth if, like some arbitrary geometry, *it disregarded experience* completely, it is not easy to see.'[2] In other words, if we were faced with the two sets of propositions which we imagined above, we could decide between them by looking to see what was real and actually the case, i.e. by appealing to experience. It would be impossible for both of two sets of mutually contradictory propositions to cover all the known facts. Now this appeal to experience to decide between the logically possible and the actual is all very well and seems very sound sense, but it implies that truth is something over and above mere coherence. A proposition's truth has to depend not merely on its relationship of entailment with other propositions, but also on what those other propositions are, i.e. on whether or not they are independently acceptable.

1. For a more detailed criticism on similar lines, see J. Wisdom, *Problems of Mind and Matter*, pp. 190–4.
2. Blanshard, op. cit., p. 276 (italics mine).

F

## 7. Further difficulty: status of the theory itself, and of the laws of logic

Similarly, the theory is in trouble over fundamental principles such as the statement of the theory itself and the laws of logic. For instance, the statement that the truth of a proposition consists in its membership of a body of mutually coherent propositions presupposes the independent truth of the laws of logic. No doubt these laws are coherent with all other true propositions, but that is not at all what we mean by saying that the laws of logic are true, nor could we say that they were false merely if we could think of no other propositions that were true. Indeed, the very meaning of 'coherence' and 'incoherence' implies the independent truth of laws such as the law of contradiction. In the sense required by the theory two propositions are incoherent if they are such that they cannot both be true. But in that very statement explaining what incoherence is we are appealing to the law of contradiction, for we are saying that certain pairs of propositions are such that they cannot both be true. And the argument that we can establish such laws as the necessary condition of our coherent system is hardly valid, for although we may appear to be establishing them by showing them to be coherent with this (or any other) system we are in fact making use of a further principle, namely, that what is the necessary condition of any coherent system is true. But how could we know, merely by the coherence test, that that itself is true?

## 8. Two different kinds of coherence being confused

Finally, it seems questionable whether the word 'coherence' is always the name for the same relation, although that it is always the name for the same relation is an assumption or an assertion which the theory makes. The theory asserts that what is incoherent cannot be true. But no proposition can by itself be either coherent or incoherent, for coherence is a relation requiring at least two terms. A proposition can be true if incoherent with some propositions, although not if incoherent with some others. Certainly, coherence makes a useful and dependable criterion of truth, provided that it is not the only criterion. The theory itself seems to slur over this point by confusing (a) the relation of coherence between a proposition

and a body of propositions with (b) the relation of coherence between
a proposition and observation.

It is far from obvious that the relation is the same in either case,
even if it is admitted that observation is propositional in character.
We use the test provided in (a) much of the time, but regard its
results as reliable only because in the end it relies on the test provided
in (b). A proposition is accepted under (a) not just because there is
another body of propositions which entail it or make it probable,
but because those propositions themselves, or others underlying
them, have been accepted under (b). The theory would not deny
that—indeed, as we saw in the last quotation, it insists on it—but it
appears to suppose that the relation is in each case the same. But
the relation between

    (i) the proposition, 'This disc is red', and
    (ii) the observation of the red disc,
is surely as different as it could be from the relation between

    (i) the proposition, 'This disc is red,' and
    (iii) the proposition, 'This disc is either red or not red; and it is
not not red'.
(iii) logically entails (i), and that it does is what is meant by saying
that (i) is coherent with (iii). But (ii) does not logically entail (i), for
an observation, however propositional, does not entail anything.[1] If,
on the other hand, a distinction is drawn between

    (ii) the observation of the red disc, and
    (iv) the fact of the disc being red,
we should have to say, according to the theory, that (iv) is in principle
unobservable; and we should then have no ground for supposing
that the relation between (i) and (iv) was at all like that between (i)
and (iii), and consequently none for giving them the same name
'coherence'. In fact, Tweedledum and Tweedledee would once more
be united, for both Coherence and Correspondence theories would

1. That verification is propositional does not prove that it is the discovery of
the relation of coherence between the proposition to be verified and a body of
already accepted propositions. It will still be the relation between the proposition
and what the verifying observation discovers. What it discovers may only be
intelligible in the light of past experience, but it is not the same as past experience;
and all experience, including past experience, is experience of something other
than experience.

164 Theory of Knowledge

be asserting a mysterious relation between proposition and fact, and each would be giving it a private name.

### 9. Truth is identity of proposition and fact

What positively emerges from this lengthy discussion of the two main theories, which appears to have been so negative? Both theories agree that truth is a relation between a proposition (taking the relevant meaning of 'judgment' on the Coherence theory to be the same as 'proposition') and something else. How far they differ on the two questions (*a*) what is the relation? and (*b*) to what does this relation relate the proposition? does not appear to be quite as obvious as supporters of either view would have us believe. The basic dilemma of both theories was how to give a satisfactory answer to the one question which would not rule out the possibility of a satisfactory answer to the other. If Coherence makes the mode of verification purely propositional it may be enabled to answer clearly what the truth relation is, i.e. in its pure form a relation of logical entailment between propositions, but it is then giving an answer such that we can never get outside the circle of propositions; and the difficulties of dualism surge over us once more. The problem for Correspondence, on the other hand, was how clearly to distinguish between propositions and facts, so as in turn to explain what the relation of correspondence holding between them, in the case of true propositions, could be. Obviously enough, some distinction was needed for reasons already sufficiently explained, in particular to allow for the possibility of error and false propositions. But does this once more lead back to a dualism of proposition and fact, to a rigid dichotomy of the two realms? Although we must certainly make error possible, for it is unfortunately actual enough, I rather doubt whether such a provision requires us to accept the divorce of proposition and fact which Correspondence assumes.

The scheme of Correspondence may briefly be summarized thus:

(i) For judgment, including false judgment, to be possible at all we need propositions and facts.

(ii) Truth will be some relation which does hold between true propositions and facts, but which does not hold between false propositions and facts.

(iii) The relation required is correspondence.

I would accept (i) and (ii), but would suggest that (iii) is both unnecessary and false, and that instead the relation required is the simple relation of numerical identity (interpreting identity as a relation for these purposes). What, we may ask, is the difference between a true proposition and a fact? What, for instance, is the difference between the proposition expressed by the sentence, 'The cat is on the mat', and the fact that the cat is on the mat? What need have we *both* of true propositions *and* of facts? It is only if we assume both that we have to start looking for some relation to tie them together. And I suspect that we are only tempted to want both because we assume that there are *things* called propositions or, for the matter of that, *things* called facts. We saw earlier that although it was convenient to talk of the contents of judgment in terms of propositions,[1] it did not require us to suppose that there were special entities called propositions, and that the theory which supposes that there are runs into serious difficulties. If, then, there is no such entity as a proposition, the relation of correspondence which is offered as the nature of truth must be of a very Pickwickian sort.

Here we run into the obvious objection in the way of suggesting that there is no difference between a true proposition and a fact, namely, that although, as has been admitted, there would be no propositions at all, let alone true propositions, if there were no minds, there would be facts, i.e. that while propositions are mind-dependent facts are not. But is it really so clear that facts are independent of minds? Certainly, we ordinarily disagree with that form of idealism which is especially associated with Berkeley, and we suppose that if suddenly all minds in the world ceased to exist a number of things might go on happening in just the same way that they happen now. The cat might still be sitting on the mat, in the tropics the sun would still melt ice at sea level, and if two apples were blown off a tree followed by a third three apples would have fallen off the tree. That is, we suppose that events would go on occurring, and that a number of events would exhibit common features, repeatable patterns, etc. In that sense facts are not dependent on minds.

1. ch. 5.

But here the appalling, though perhaps convenient, looseness of our usage of the word 'fact' comes in. When we say that facts cannot be mind-dependent because even if there were no minds many facts might still go on as before, do we mean that many *events* would occur belonging to the same natural kinds as many of the events which now occur? or do we mean that certain propositions, if formulated, would be true? *Ex hypothesi* they cannot be formulated, for there are no minds to do the job, but that does not affect the truth (or otherwise) of the statement that if they were formulated they would be true. In the first case, in saying that some facts are independent of minds we mean that some events are; and in the second case we are saying that the truth of a proposition depends on something independent of the mind that formulates it. In the first case the alleged difference between a proposition and a fact has become the difference between a proposition and an event, which is not denied but is here irrelevant; and in the second case the alleged difference is seen to be unreal. Or, again, facts may be represented as abstractions, not quite from events, for they themselves are in their way abstractions, too, but from the whole process of world history; and false propositions will then be bits of facts wrongly combined by the judging mind, true propositions bits of fact correctly combined.

We could, indeed, eliminate the word 'fact' from the language altogether, and substitute for it the longer expression, 'true proposition'. 'Fact' and 'true proposition' are certainly logically equivalent, by which is meant that wherever a statement involving the one is true a statement involving the other is true also. But where two propositions, $p$ and $q$, are logically equivalent, i.e. where $p$ entails $q$ and $q$ entails $p$, it is not necessarily the case that $p$ and $q$ mean the same thing, that they are not two propositions but one. Our problem is: given that 'fact' and 'true proposition' are logically equivalent (i.e. that to any statement involving the one a statement involving the other corresponds, in the required relationship) may we also say that they are identical? In ordinary usage they surely are identical, in that whenever we assert that something is a fact we could (and often do) assert that it is true (or, more pedantically, a true proposition) without change of meaning. What is the

difference between 'Is it a fact that Hitler is dead?' and 'Is it true
that Hitler is dead?' or between 'The plain fact is that I am broke'
and 'The plain truth is that I am broke'? or between 'I know for a
fact that there were six £1 notes in my wallet' and 'I know it to be
true that there were six £1 notes in my wallet'? and so on.

As we use them, 'fact' and 'true proposition' ('true', 'truth') are
normally identical in *descriptive* meaning, i.e. what would be
asserted in the one case is the same as what would be asserted in the
other. The *emotional* meaning of sentences may vary with the
substitution of 'fact' for 'true' according to the context, and *vice
versa*. If you doubt some story which I have told you, and I wish to
impress its truth on you, I may tend to talk in terms of 'facts', as
if to suggest that what you are presuming to doubt is not some
opinion of mine (which *might* be false), but something which actually
happened and is quite independent of my personal and corrigible
opinions. On the whole, 'fact' has a tone of hardness and unavoida-
bility about it which makes it a useful word to employ when we wish
to *emphasise* the truth of what we are asserting. On the other hand,
there may be contexts (and I think there are) in which the emphasis
is more effectively conveyed by using 'true' instead of 'fact'. But the
point is that the difference is purely one of emphasis; what is being
asserted is in either case the same, and if we want to redouble the
emphasis we may employ the combination phrase, 'really and truly'.
In colloquial English we ask for confirmation of a statement indiffer-
ently by 'really?' 'is that so?' 'is that true?' etc., although some other
languages seem to concentrate chiefly on the latter, e.g. French
'*vraiment?*' and Italian '*è vero?*'

## 10. The difference between p and p is true

The conclusion that a true proposition is identical with a fact, and
therefore that truth cannot be a relation such as correspondence
between them, may be indicated from a slightly different angle. Do
we add anything to the assertion of *p* by asserting '*p* is true'? e.g.
what is the difference between 'The cat is on the mat' and '"The cat
is on the mat" is true'? In most cases it seems to me that I mean exactly
the same thing by the two statements, the addition of 'is true' in the
second being the mark of emphasis that I am asserting that the cat

is on the mat. (When you raise a doubt and I insist, 'But it's *true*, I tell you', what am I insisting? Surely that the cat is on the mat, or, if you prefer it, that the cat *is* on the mat.) Nevertheless, I am not sure that in some cases *p* and '*p* is true' are not different in meaning, and that that is not what has led many into supposing that they are always different, and consequently into looking for a correspondence or a coherence which is asserted in the one but not in the other. When I say '*p*' I am always asserting *p*. When I say '*p* is true' I may mean, 'If you assert *p*, then what you assert is true', or, 'If you want to assert what is true, assert *p*'. That is to say, while in the first case I am *actually* asserting *p*, in the second case I am *dispositionally* asserting it, or asserting a proposition about *p*, that is, a second order proposition.

Although such second order propositions are more frequently employed by philosophers than others, we do sometimes employ them as non-philosophers, for instance, in making polite circumlocutions, or in hinting at the truth where we would scruple to tell it directly; e.g. 'You wouldn't be far wrong if you were to say . . .' and other such phrases. Even in this usage, where *p* and '*p* is true' are not identical, they are still logically equivalent. Nevertheless, because they are not always identical we cannot say simply 'that the terms "true" and "false" connote nothing, but function in the sentence simply as marks of assertion and denial'.[1] In the second usage of '*p* is true' we are not simply asserting *p* or even simply asserting 'If you assert *p*, then what you assert is what I assert'. We are calling attention to the identity of a proposition and a fact which constitutes a proposition's truth, which is something that we are not doing when we assert *p*, or when in the first usage we assert '*p* is true'.

A similar account may be given of negative propositions, not-*p* or '*p* is false'. The latter may either mean exactly the same as the former, and in that case I take it to be asserting not something about *p*, but a relation of difference (e.g. '*x* is not *y*' means '*x* is other than *y*'); or it may be a second order proposition meaning, 'If you assert not-*p*, what you assert is true', or, 'If you assert *p*, what you assert is false'.

Summarily *p* is true if and only if *p*. The proposition, 'The cat is

1. A. J. Ayer, *Language, Truth and Logic*, p. 122

on the mat', is true if and only if the cat is on the mat; and if the cat *is* on the mat, then the proposition that it is is not different from the fact that it is. If this seems a disappointingly tame answer to the problem of truth, after such elaborate theories of it have been advanced and discussed, the elaborators of the theories are to blame for inventing and inflating the problem to its generally accepted proportions. We are still left with a problem of truth, but not with the problem that we looked to have on our hands at the beginning. The question now is not when is a proposition true, but when are we to believe it, i.e. a question not about the nature of truth but about the means of discovering it, about standards of acceptance, about verification. The question has a twofold aspect: (*a*) the analysis of belief (and disbelief) and knowledge, and the difference between them; and (*b*) the conditions of a belief's validity; of these (*b*) belonging to the theory of induction lies outside the scope of this book, and (*a*) will be discussed in the following chapter.

# 8

## KNOWING AND BELIEVING

### 1. Traditional distinction of knowledge and belief

The notion that our cognitive activities can be sharply divided into kinds which are fundamentally different from each other, knowing on the one hand and believing on the other, has a long philosophical history, and has endured a less chequered career than most philosophical notions of its antiquity. According to the traditional view, which derives from Plato, knowledge and belief are mental faculties, each *sui generis*, no more to be defined one in terms of the other than are, say, love and friendship. They are, indeed, allied, as love and friendship are allied, and they are more like each other than either is to, say, doubt or love or desire. They are alike in that what a man knows he will express in the form of an assertion or denial, and that what he believes he will similarly express. Again, from many of a man's statements one cannot tell without further questioning whether what he asserts is something which he claims to know or something which he claims to believe.

If a man is very careful he will say, 'I know it is raining' (and perhaps even there he is not being careful enough), or 'I believe Black Beauty will win the 2.30'. But more often than not he will say, 'It is raining', or 'Black Beauty will win the 2.30'. Knowledge and belief then resemble each other in that what is known or believed is normally expressible in an assertion or denial ('John of Gaunt hasn't a hope against Black Beauty'), which does not contain the words 'know' or 'believe' or their equivalents. On the other hand, the expression of a doubt (in the sense of not being willing to commit oneself either way) cannot be made without either saying, 'I doubt . . .' or without using a phrase which operates in an equivalent way, such as 'may or may not', 'just possibly', and so on.

But although they are alike in that respect, a respect which might roughly be covered by calling them both judging faculties, knowledge and belief have been held to be otherwise different in kind. We might and do confuse them, for a man can think he knows when he does not, but nevertheless according to this view they are not adjacent portions on a single scale, so that one merges into the other across a borderline which may be shadowy, shifting, and conventional. About the exact distinction between them philosophers who have maintained that they are generically different activities have not always been as clear or helpful as could be wished. To say, for instance, that in knowing the mind apprehends facts, but in believing it has propositions for its objects, is, as our earlier discussion of facts and propositions should have indicated, totally uninformative, and is merely a more long-winded way of saying that in knowing one knows, but in believing one believes.

Perhaps the distinction which is mainly, although by no means without exception, adhered to is one which again goes back to Plato: that the only things a man may know are necessary truths, such as the truths of mathematics or of logic, while all else can at best be a matter of belief. I may then know that two Euclidean triangles having the same base and between the same parallels are equal in area, and I may know that if $A$ is larger than $B$ and if $B$ is larger than $C$, then $A$ is larger than $C$. They, it is held, are necessary truths which could not conceivably be otherwise, which a man has only to understand to perceive that they must be true. On the other hand, most of what commonly passes for knowledge is strictly not knowledge at all—both singular pieces, as that you are now reading a book which I have written, that you had two cups of tea for breakfast this morning, and that in 1950 Easter Sunday fell on April 9; and general pieces, as that bottles thrown out of the window fall downwards, not upwards (or more generally still, that material objects attract each other), that unnecessary pulling of the communication cord on an English railway train renders the offender liable to a fine, and that most cricketers bat right-handed.

These propositions are not the objects of knowledge, not because they are not true (for they well may be, and the theory is not concerned to deny that they are), but because they are contingent truths, which might conceivably be false. They carry no guarantee which provides 100 per cent insurance against their being false; and if they might conceivably be false, however remote the possibility may be, they cannot be the objects of knowledge, for knowledge cannot be wrong. Impressed with the uncertified character of contingent propositions, Descartes attempted by a systematic scrutiny to find some strict knowledge which would underwrite them, valiantly but signally failed, and by his failure led on to Hume's insistence on the uncertain character of all matter-of-fact beliefs, a form of scepticism which recent preoccupation with problems of perception has done much to perpetuate.

## 2. Knowledge and belief as dispositions

That this traditional division of cognition into two essentially different kinds, knowledge and belief, is false and rests on a confusion I hope to show in what follows. But there is another mistake which is attributed to the theory, and which I do not propose to discuss, although in a more detailed study it could not be avoided. Knowing and believing have been spoken of above as activities, and that, or something like it, is the way they are normally and perhaps thoughtlessly spoken of. This naturally leads to (or perhaps itself leads from) thinking of knowing something (and correspondingly for belief) as a mental act which has a certain object and which occurs at a certain time. The reason may well be that because 'know' is a transitive verb governing an accusative we tend in our thought to assimilate knowing to other acts which are named by transitive verbs governing themselves.

Take the case of hitting, for example. If we hear that A has hit B, we may want to ask when he hit him, or how long he continued to hit him. Hitting is an event or a process, about which it is sense to ask when it occurred or when it started and how long it lasted. But we cannot ask the corresponding things about knowing. Knowing and believing are not properly to be called acts at all, but are dispositional in character. That is, it does not have to be the case that some event is now going on in my mind, or that I am performing some mental act, for it to be the case that I know (as I do) that six nines are fifty-four, or that a Communist *coup* succeeded in Czechoslovakia at the end of February 1948. My daughter believes that I am clever at mending things, although she is not now thinking of that. My wife knows that milk boils over easily, although she is not now thinking of it, and although she almost never thinks of it when she is boiling milk.

Nevertheless, to say that knowledge and belief are not activities or states but dispositions is not the whole story, for there is such an occurrence as coming to know and coming to believe (' I suddenly realised . . .', 'It was only when she blushed that I believed she was lying', etc.). That is, it is sense to ask questions such as, 'When did you first know . . . ?' and 'When did you cease to believe . . . ?' And although they may be interpreted as questions asking when certain dispositions were initiated, these dispositions are initiated by something happening, and by that something happening to the person who thereafter knows or who thereafter no longer believes, e.g. the woman who thought her blouse was white until she saw her neighbour's. Whatever realising, ceasing to believe, etc., may be, they are certainly events involving minds. And therefore, although it may be, as I think it is, correct to insist on the dispositional nature of knowledge and belief, that does not automatically dispose of the problems which worried philosophers who wrongly thought of knowing and believing as acts of different and special sorts. With that proviso, therefore, and without the need to attempt an analysis of what a disposition is, we may return to our main problem of determining the difference between knowledge and belief.

## 3. *Distinction between* a priori *and empirical propositions*

As already indicated, the traditional insistence on a difference in kind between all knowing and all believing is closely connected with the traditional distinction between *a priori* and empirical propositions, the first being held to be knowable, but the second only believable. The distinction between *a priori* and empirical propositions, and its relevance to the supposed difference in kind between knowledge and belief, can be pointed out in two ways, both emphasising the necessity of *a priori* propositions and the contingency of empirical propositions. First, there is the difference already referred to, that a true *a priori* proposition could not conceivably be false. The proposition expressed by the sentence '3 + 4 = 7' is, as a proposition of pure mathematics, a proposition of this kind; no state of this or any other world is conceivable in which that proposition might be false. We might, of course, alter our symbolism in English so as to use the character '2' where we have hitherto written '4', and thenceforth it would be correct to say '3 + 2 = 7'. But what we should then mean by '3 + 2 = 7' would be exactly what we now mean by ' 3 + 4 = 7', and not what we now mean by '3 + 2 = 7'.

Continuing to use our present symbolism, the sentence '3 + 4 = 7' expresses a necessary truth, and that 7 is not the sum of 3 plus 4 is necessarily false. On the other hand, that the earth rotates on its axis from west to east is a hypothesis which might conceivably be false. It is simply a matter of empirical fact that it does spin that way. It is, that is, an exceedingly well established hypothesis, so well established that for practical purposes it can be accepted as a piece of knowledge, but there is no necessity about it. We can easily conceive its spinning from east to west. That is, whereas '3 + 2 = 7' could only be made true by a change in our linguistic usage, and the fact expressed by that sentence would be the same as the fact previously expressed by the sentence '3 + 4 = 7','The earth spins from east to west' could be made true by a change in the behaviour of the earth.

The second way of emphasising the difference between *a priori* and empirical propositions is to point out the difference in our mode of establishing them. Once we grasp the truth of an *a priori* proposition we do not look for further evidence in its favour, and we do not, indeed, treat fresh instances or applications of it as evidence at all. We would not say that a man's knowledge of 3 + 4 = 7 was in any way improved or better established by his coming across more and more cases of a trio and a quartet adding up to a septet. We may, in fact, learn some *a priori* truths that way. I am sure, for instance, that I first learned that the angle subtended by the diameter of a circle at any point on the circumference is a right-angle by drawing a number of diagrams and measuring (or guessing at) the angle in each case;

and that only later did I discover or was I taught the demonstrative proof of that conclusion, making use of already established knowledge of the properties of isosceles triangles. But once it was established by demonstration within the system of Euclid there was no need for me to go on collecting instances; the conclusion being certain, the collection of fresh evidence could do nothing to improve its certainty.

On the other hand, if we take an empirical generalisation such as 'All horses are herbivorous', we find that it was not only learned inductively, but that it is only to be established or validated inductively, too. The more horses we come across and find to be herbivorous, the more evidence we accumulate in favour of our generalisation, and the greater its probability becomes. Our confidence in the truth of an empirical generalisation is increased by the addition of further instances or applications of it, in a way in which our confidence in an *a priori* proposition is not increased by the addition of further instances or applications of it.

### 4. The corresponding distinction between knowledge and belief is false

Now, how does this affect the issue between knowledge and belief? Simply in this way, that empirical propositions are held not to be objects of knowledge because they are not necessary, and because they are only established as probabilities, of however high a degree. There is always, however remote, a possibility of an empirical proposition being false, and therefore it cannot truthfully be said to be known; for we reserve knowledge for certainties, for what cannot be false. This dubitability, or possibility of being false, infects *all* empirical propositions, and not merely the generalisations such as 'All horses are herbivorous', in which one gives a pledge to the future.

It applies equally to statements about the present ('I am now in Oxford') as to statements about the future ('The sun will rise in the east tomorrow'), and to statements about the past ('Rommel suffered from desert sores'). It applies to my supposed presence in Oxford, because however many tests I may apply to determine whether I am in Oxford, there is still the possibility that I am the victim of an elaborate hoax, which my tests have not been sufficient to find out: I *might*, for all I know, have been transported during my sleep last night to another city built exactly like Oxford in all respects. We say we know that Rommel suffered from desert sores, because we have a collection of evidence that he did; but do we know? There is the possibility that although all concerned, including the doctors, believed that he had desert sores, they were wrong, for he had some other very similar complaint; and there are other possibilities which could easily be multiplied.

These illustrations should be enough to show the difference which, it is held, lies between knowledge and belief. Knowledge is, on this view, confined to demonstrative systems, and is a goal at which belief may aim but which, although it may come closer and closer, it can never quite attain. Belief, bound however lightly by the ties of contingency and probability, is different in kind from knowledge, firmly enclosed within the circle of certainty.[1]

Now, as I said earlier, this rigid distinction is false and rests on a confusion, which is none the less a confusion for being easily made. Because knowledge is of what is true, and of what could not possibly

---

1. This *a priori*-empirical view of the antithesis between knowledge and belief is liable to be confused with another, by which all propositions are divided up into incorrigible and corrigible. On this view knowledge will have for its field the province of what is incorrigible, and included in that province will be some empirical propositions, which have been variously referred to as basic, or primitive, or protocol propositions. It has been held, for example, that although I may be wrong in supposing that what I see is a table, I cannot be wrong in supposing that it looks like a table; or, in other terminology, although I may wrong in supposing that I am perceiving a green material object, I cannot be wrong in supposing that I sense a green sense datum. Thus some empirical propositions are in a way necessary propositions (although not logically necessary, not *a priori*), and these, but not others, may be known. On this distinction, various theories of knowing, or of knowing of one kind, as being a non-inferential acquaintance, are constructed. I do not discuss them in this chapter because I cannot accept the distinction itself. I may be less likely to make a mistake in supposing that what I see looks like a table than in supposing that it is a table, or in supposing that I am sensing a green sense datum than in supposing that I perceive a green leaf. But there is nothing especially privileged about the first alternative in either case. I am, of course, very unlikely to be wrong if I play for safety by supposing anything so vague as that a sense datum is green. But if I am more precise and suppose it to be emerald green or avocado green or leaf green, I can and often do go wrong (and wrong not only about words). And that is a matter of common enough experience to justify passing over here a view about knowledge which depends on denying it.

be false, and because, in the case of an empirical proposition, there is some possibility of its being false, it is concluded that empirical propositions cannot be known, but can only at best be truly believed. But that argument involves confusing two different notions of possibility. The sense in which a necessary truth could not possibly be false is the sense of logical possibility; it is logically impossible for 3 + 4 to equal 8, if '3 + 4 = 8' is interpreted as an *a priori* proposition. If all horses are herbivorous, and if Brown Jack is a horse, then it is logically impossible for Brown Jack not to be herbivorous. Whether or not we can know that all horses are herbivorous, we can know that if all horses are herbivorous, and if Brown Jack is a horse, then Brown Jack is herbivorous; and what we there know is as good an *a priori* necessity as what we know in knowing that 3 + 4 = 7. In that sense of 'possible', it is always possible that an empirical proposition is false. It is not logically impossible that the sun will rise in the west tomorrow, or that water freezes at 50 degrees Fahrenheit.

But although there is a logical possibility of an empirical proposition being false—that there is such a possibility is part of what is meant by calling it an *empirical* proposition—there is another sense of possible, in which it is not possible for some empirical propositions to be false. In this sense there is no possibility that Gandhi was not murdered, that I am not now in Oxford, that the sun will rise in the west tomorrow. Take another instance: you are, you suppose, now sitting in your chair reading this book, and it occurs to you to try doubting whether you are sitting in your chair reading this book. How would you set about clearing up the doubt, removing the possibility of your being wrong? You would do it, of course, by pinching yourself to test whether you were awake, by feeling the chair, by getting up and looking at it, by sitting down in it again, by trying to put your fist through the book and failing, by asking the man opposite if this was a book and that was a chair, and so on, for as long as you like. Can you, after passing all those tests, doubt that this is a book and that that is a chair? If so, it is not a doubt that any empirical tests, however successful and however long continued, will remove; and if it is not that sort of a doubt, what sort of a doubt is it? The plain fact is that if you, the chair, and the book all pass the above tests (which could be indefinitely extended, although in practice you would be satisfied with far fewer), then there is no possibility of your being mistaken, and you know that you are sitting in the chair reading the book. On the other hand, you only believe that your wife is out playing bridge because, although she is out and although she usually does play bridge on this afternoon in the week, she sometimes goes to the cinema instead; there is, then, a real possibility that she is at the cinema. You know what you are now doing, but you do not know what she is now doing.

### 5. *Knowledge not confined to what is necessarily true*

What the view which we are criticising is asking us to do is to confine the word 'know' to *necessary* facts, on the ground that if a fact is not necessary there is some possibility of its not being a fact. But there is no possibility of its not being a fact, and it is absurd to suggest that there might be. Knowledge is certainly of what cannot possibly be other than what it is, but, as I have tried to show, possibility is certainly an ambiguous and, I think, also a vague notion. That you are not now reading this book is logically possible, in that the proposition that you are not now reading this book is not self-contradictory. But there is no possibility that you are not now reading this book, and you know it. There may be a possibility that you will immediately give up reading it, but not that you are not now reading it. When there is no possibility that $x$ is not occurring, then you may know that $x$ is occurring; and although philosophically determining the conditions of the presence or absence of such a possibility may prove difficult, we normally have no difficulty in practice in recognising its absence or presence. There is, then, no solid case for maintaining that knowing is confined within demonstrative systems.

We can put the matter, if we like, by saying that there is more than one sense of the word 'know'. But we only make fools of ourselves if we try to pretend that we do not really know such things as that Gandhi was murdered, that World War II ended in 1945, that Frenchmen talk a different language from Englishmen, that aeroplanes travel faster than snails, and so on. Not merely do we know such facts, and thousands of others like them, but we learned how to use the word 'know' precisely with reference to such facts. Extending it to refer to necessary truths comes at a later and normally unnoticed stage, unnoticed because the distinction between necessary and contingent truths is a sophisticated distinction which few men have any occasion to make.

### 6. *Knowledge and belief may have the same objects*

So far, then, we have seen that knowledge cannot be distinguished from belief by a difference in their objects. We may distinguish necessary from contingent or empirical truths, but we have no right to say that the latter cannot be objects of knowledge. Again, there seems no solid ground for denying that we can have successively belief and knowledge of the same objects, both in the case of necessary and in the case of contingent truths. During the period when I was drawing my diagrams of the angles subtended by the diameter of a circle at points on the circumference I came to hold the belief that all such angles were right-angles; and, later, when I learned the proof, I came to know that all such angles were right-angles. I believe there is a house on fire somewhere in the district when I hear the clanging of the fire bells and see the fire engines dash past my window; I know there is a house on fire somewhere in the district when, having pursued the fire engines, I find them outside a blazing house, with the crews pumping water on to the flames. Normally the passage of thought is from belief to knowledge: one starts with belief and later (but not, of course, always) arrives at knowledge. That is, belief, when it is confirmed, becomes knowledge.

Exactly the reverse process is not possible: we cannot say that knowledge, when it is infirmed (i.e. shown not to be certain), becomes belief, because our notion of knowledge (or our usage of 'knowledge') prevents us speaking that way. Our notion of knowledge is such that a man does not know something unless what he knows is not only true but certainly true; consequently, if what a man once took to be certainly true is shown not to be certainly true, we would not say that he formerly knew it but now only believed it; we might say that formerly he *thought* he knew, but that he must have been wrong in thinking so, because what he thought he knew is not certainly true, and therefore cannot be said to be known.

Nevertheless, there is a different process by which knowledge can relapse into belief, namely, through forgetfulness or losing the evidence. My geometrical example again will serve: when searching my mind for an instance to illustrate my statement on p. 174 that an *a priori* truth can be learned inductively, I hit on that one. But, because in the last twenty years I have had no occasion to think about angles subtended by diameters, not only had I forgotten how to prove that they were right-angles, but I was not even *quite* sure that it was true that they were right-angles, although I was strongly inclined to think so. I was, therefore, in the position of believing what I once knew (although I could not at the time of believing it know that I once knew). This belief has now once more been converted into knowledge, by my remembering what I had forgotten, namely, how to prove the theorem. My history with reference to the truth of that theorem, then, is that at one period I believed it, later I knew it, later again I believed it, and now once more I know it. I see no good reason for supposing that my present knowledge will not rapidly lapse into belief.

### 7. *That one knows is not discovered by introspection*

We tend to talk of knowing and believing as activities or states of mind. But it should now be clear that whether or not one can determine the character of some so-called states of mind by introspection, one cannot tell by introspection whether a given state of mind is one of knowing. If on claiming to know that your wife is in the kitchen your claim is challenged, you cannot tell introspectively (and you are not, in fact, tempted to try finding out that way) whether you really do know. So-called examining your mind to find out whether you do know (except, perhaps, in the case of memory) is most unlike examining your mind to find out whether your present feeling is one of regret or of remorse. You can, perhaps, tell introspectively whether you are sure of something, if being sure consists of having a present feeling of conviction. But even there there is a risk of ambiguity, because normally when you are asked the question 'Are you sure'?, as you might be when you claimed to know that your wife was in the kitchen, you do not take the question to be an invitation to examine or measure a feeling of conviction, but you take it as invitation to re-examine the proposition which you claimed to know, together with the relevant evidence, to determine whether you are still sure, and whether you would still claim to know.

If, having asserted that it is raining, you are asked whether you are sure, you take the question to be an invitation to look out of the window again, and perhaps more carefully than before. 'Are you sure?' has other meanings, too, and may, for instance, be an invitation, not to re-examine the proposition and the evidence for it, but to express your confidence, e.g. by making a bet. 'How sure are you?' is often and correctly answered by saying how much one is prepared to bet on the proposition being true. In short, we can never determine by introspection whether we know, and we seldom try to determine by introspection whether we are sure.

## 8. Differences between knowing and being sure

That, however they may be related, knowing and being sure are different can be shown by two quite simple considerations. First, one can be sure and be wrong, but one cannot know and be wrong. From the fact that you are sure that it is raining it does not follow that it is raining, but from the fact that you know that it is raining it does follow that it is raining. It does not, of course, follow from the fact that you *say* that you know it is raining; for you may say you know and be wrong about that, for you do not know. If a man says he is sure it is raining (and if we do not suppose that he is lying) and we discover that it is, in fact, not raining, we say that he was sure but he was wrong. But if he said not that he was sure but that he knew that it was raining, and we discovered that it was not raining, then we should say that he *thought* he knew but he was wrong. In the first case, we do not say, 'He *thought* he was sure, but he was not sure'[1] (to be contrasted with the fact that we do say, 'He *thought* he knew, but he did not know'); and in the second case we do not say, 'He knew, but he was wrong' (to be contrasted with the fact that we do say, 'He was sure, but he was wrong').

1. We do sometimes say that a man thought he was sure, but he was not sure, but not on the ground that what he was sure of turned out to be false; what he thought he was sure of might indeed even turn out to be true. e.g. a man might say that he was sure that he could perform a certain trick and yet by the way he tackled the trick show that he was not sure, even though he succeeded in doing it.

A second difference between knowing and being sure is that to say, 'I know that . . .' offers a guarantee in a way in which to say, 'I am sure that . . .' does not. Suppose at a party you ask me who is the man talking to our hostess and I reply that it is Dr Brown, and suppose that in response to further enquiries from you (for you do not know Dr Brown, but have long been anxious to meet him) I insist that I know it is Dr Brown. If, on the strength of that, you introduce yourself to him and find that he is not Dr Brown at all, you would then round on me for unreliability in a way in which you might be less inclined to round on me if I had only said that I was sure that the man was Dr Brown. Saying that I know both pledges myself in a way that saying I am sure does not, and also emphasises that what I say that I know is a hard, impersonal fact which is quite independent of me. Saying that I am sure does not offer the same 100 per cent guarantee, and does not insist on the dissociation of the fact from myself.[1] Again, one is ready to qualify sureness (I'm pretty sure . . . not quite sure . . . almost sure', etc.) in a way in which one is not prepared to qualify knowledge.

Nevertheless, being sure is necessary to knowledge, for it would not be sense to say, 'I know that it is raining, but I am not quite sure of it.'[2] We may, therefore, say so far that knowing involves:

(i) that what is known is true;

(ii) that the person knowing is sure that it is true.

However, although these are necessary conditions, they are not yet sufficient, for it would not be difficult to think of situations in which both conditions were fulfilled and yet one could not truly be said to know. For instance, Professor Hubble may be sure that the universe is expanding at a speed higher than that of any normal explosion, and he may be right, but he does not know that the universe is expanding at that speed; for the data which he has observed, namely, the shift towards red of the light of remote

1. This certifying or guaranteeing character of 'I know that . . .' is clearly brought out in a discussion by J. L. Austin in *Supplementary Proceedings of the Aristotelian Society*, vol. xx, pp. 170–4.

2. In a later article I came to disagree with the view expressed here that being sure is necessary to knowing: 'Knowing and Not Knowing' (*Proceedings of the Aristotelian Society*, 1952–3). Cf. also articles by G. J. Warnock and L. J. Cohen (*Supplementary Proceedings of the Aristotelian Society*, 1962).

nebulae, are consistent with alternative hypotheses to his own. Or a pessimist may be sure that it will rain tonight because he is giving a large fireworks party, and he may turn out to be right, for it does rain tonight, but he would hardly be said to have known that it would rain. On reading a newspaper report of the prosecutions case in a murder trial I may be sure that the defendant will be found guilty, and I may be right (for he is subsequently found guilty), but I certainly do not know that he will be found guilty; for that I should at least require to have heard or to have read a fair summary of the case for the defence, quite apart from questions about the impartiality or the sound judgment of the jury.

## 9. Conditions of knowledge

If $p$ is the proposition in question, then a man does not know $p$, even although he is sure of $p$, and although $p$ is true, in any of the following conditions:

    (*a*) he has no evidence for $p$;

    (*b*) he is wrong about the evidence;

    (*c*) he is wrong about the relation of the evidence to $p$.

The pessimist who claims to know that his fireworks party will be spoiled by rain does not know, because he has no evidence for saying that it will be so spoiled; he comes under condition (*a*). Conditions (*b*) and (*c*) concern mistakes about evidence, but mistakes of different kinds. Mistakes under (*b*) consist of being misinformed about the data which one is using as evidence, e.g. as the sky grows darker, taking it to be due to the piling up of rain clouds, when it is, in fact, due to clouds of smoke from oil storage tanks on fire; I might under that misapprehension unjustifiably predict that rain would spoil my fireworks party tonight. The astronomer would be making a similar mistake if he supposed that the light from the distant nebulae showed a red shift, when actually it did not; and the newspaper reader would be making a similar mistake if he supposed, on reading the heading, 'Queen Elizabeth Held Up By Breakdown', that the liner had been delayed, when in fact the train in which the Queen of England was travelling had been held up by a breakdown farther along the line. The astronomer could not, in such circumstances, know that the universe was expanding at the speed of an explosion (even although he was right, and it was); and the newspaper reader could not know that the liner would dock at Southampton behind schedule (even although he was right, and it would).

Mistakes under (c) are probably more common. Here one is wrong not about the evidence itself, but about its function *as* evidence, about its relation to the conclusion, either because it is not evidence for the conclusion, or because, although it is evidence for the conclusion, it is not sufficient.

An instance of the first would be an accusation of forgery built up on a hasty comparison of two signatures and the supposition that they were written by the same man, when a more careful scrutiny would have shown that they were not. An instance of the second (more common than the first) would be a charge of murder depending on the presence of the defendant's fingerprints on the door handle of the room in which the body was found; the fingerprints are certainly some evidence, but far from sufficient, for several other people might have had occasion to visit the room at about the time of the murder, each with as good a motive for committing the murder as the defendant had; and in order to point suspicion towards the defendant (who certainly did visit the room) the others might have been careful to wear gloves or not to touch the door handle. In each of these two cases the charges might be correct, for the defendants did commit respectively the forgery and the murder, but in neither case could it be known from the facts mentioned above as evidence that the defendants were guilty.

To know, then, a man must

(a) have evidence;

(b) be right about the evidence; and

(c) be right about the relation of the evidence to the conclusion.

He must also be sure that he is right under (b) and (c). It is not necessary to knowing *p* that the man should go through a long and explicit process of self-questioning under (b) and (c). A man's claim to know that Gandhi is dead is legitimate if he *can* now prove it; it is not necessary that he should just *have* proved it.

## 10. Conditions of belief

We may now turn to belief, supplementing what has so far been said about knowledge; and in the light of the earlier discussion what follows can be put fairly shortly. Believing *p* consists in a combination of the following two points: (i) being prepared to say Yes to the question *p*? with varying degrees of conviction; and (ii) having some evidence for *p*. Where an increase in conviction is produced by an increase in the evidence (and evidence can increase in more than one dimension) the belief is rational. We would call irrational the belief that it will rain tonight simply because one has arranged a fireworks party, and rational the belief that it will rain tonight because the official weather forecasts predict rain for tonight. Belief may wander throughout the whole range of rationality and irrationality, according to the extent, nature, and value of the evidence, but I do not think we ever believe, if there is a total absence of anything which one would regard as evidence (even though one might be quite wrong in so regarding it).

One may in some cases have to act as if one believed, e.g. deciding on a batting order of a cricket team, knowing nothing of any of the players' ability; but being prepared to act as if one believes is different from believing, and acting as if one believes is different from acting because one believes. There are, too, cases where one 'has a hunch', or when one is blindly confident, but would feel hard put to it to produce any evidence. But here, I think, the feeling of difficulty is due not to consciousness of inability to produce the evidence, but to a consciousness of its comparative or total worthlessness as evidence if produced. One therefore takes refuge in blind hunches or in insisting that 'it is my lucky day'.

Increase in rational belief may become (and often does become) knowledge, namely, when the evidence increases to the point of becoming conclusive. Whether there is a genuine problem about when evidence in general becomes conclusive, it is not my business to discuss. I am inclined to think there is not, and I am certain that even if there is it cannot be a problem such that until it is solved we have no justification for saying that we have conclusive evidence in particular cases. We do have conclusive evidence for a vast number of empirical propositions, singular, particular, and general, and when we have conclusive evidence for a proposition we know it to be true.

Belief, then, covers the following five cases:

(i) Being sure and being right, on evidence which is not conclusive.

(ii) Being sure and being wrong, on evidence which is not conclusive.

(iii) Being unsure and being right, on evidence which is not conclusive.

(iv) Being unsure and being wrong, on evidence which is not conclusive.

(v) Being unsure and being right, on evidence which is conclusive.

The final case,[1] namely

(vi) Being sure and being right, on evidence which is conclusive, is the case not of believing, but of knowing. Knowing $p$, then, will consist of surely believing $p$ where $p$ is true, and of the belief being due to having conclusive evidence for $p$. Having conclusive evidence for $p$ will consist either in explicitly attending to it and consciously treating it as evidence, inferring $p$ from it, or in being able, if called on, to attend to it explicitly, etc., i.e. in the possibility of inferring $p$. Knowledge has thus been analysed, not as something generically different from belief, but as the limiting case of belief, something which belief becomes when the evidence is good enough.

Because I do not know that it is logically impossible (indeed I know that it is logically possible) for the thing in front of me which looks like a telephone not to be a telephone, it does not follow that I do not know that it is a telephone. In fact, I do know that it is a telephone, because it bears the marks by which I have always distinguished my telephone, and because I have just used it as a telephone. If suddenly it *should* vanish or I *should* see standing in its place a radio which I have never seen before, I should be extremely surprised. I should wonder how it could have disappeared, or how a radio could have been substituted for it without my noticing. I might even wonder whether a radio had been substituted for it, or whether it had turned into a radio. But I should not doubt, nor have reason to doubt, that what had been there until this minute was a telephone. I know, in fact, that the telephone is not going to play any such tricks on me, but even if I did not know that I

1. There are two other possible combinations, but neither is applicable here.

should still know that it was a telephone, the evidence being what it is.

From this account it follows that the tests of knowledge and belief are twofold. The first concerns what is known or believed; if that is false, it must be belief; if it is true, the test is indecisive as between knowledge and belief. The second concerns the person involved; if he is sure on conclusive evidence, it is knowledge. It is therefore wrong to think of knowledge and belief simply as states of mind. They are partly states of mind (or, preferably, dispositions), but the difference between them may be non-mental, as the object is true or false, or mental as the subject is sure or unsure, or partly mental and partly non-mental as the subject's attitude is due to conclusive or inconclusive evidence. For either knowledge or belief to exist one member out of each of these three pairs of factors must be present. Only when the first member of each pair is present do we have knowledge, and in all other combinations we have belief.

# INDEX